To one of the fine~~st~~ _____ ever to wear a Tulsa firefighers uniform, & one of the finest gentlemen I've ever had the pleasure to know:

Bob, this book, hopefully has a few laughs in store for you, and probably a little too much pontificating, but I hope you enjoy the read.

truly, when I think of TFD, I think of your skills over the radio, & how much it meant to Henry Lile & me to respond with the units we heard you dispatch.

Best wishes, always.

Bob Losure

August 3, 2002

Five to Air Seconds

In Memoriam

DON HARRISON
1936–1998

He was the heart and soul of Headline News, and his kind spirit showed in each life he touched. His deep bass voice had boomed out across America each morning since Headline News had begun in 1982. He had fought cancer twice before and won. The third time, he battled it like the valiant champion he was, until the end came in May 1998. His legacy will live on forever.

*Broadcast Journalism
Behind the Scenes*

BOB LOSURE

HILLSBORO PRESS
Franklin, Tennessee

Printed in the United States of America

02   01   00   99   98   1   2   3   4   5

Library of Congress Catalog Card Number: 98-66552

ISBN: 1-57736-107-5

Dust jacket and cover design by Gary Bozeman

Cover photo courtesy of Jeff Bach

Published by
HILLSBORO PRESS
an imprint of
PROVIDENCE HOUSE PUBLISHERS
238 Seaboard Lane • Franklin, Tennessee 37067
800-321-5692

To my mother

LARAMA MATTIE LOSURE

who at eighty-nine years young

is still an inspiring example

of the triumph of the human spirit.

# Contents

Acknowledgments

FIRST OF ALL, MY HUMBLEST THANKS TO DR. ALAN KELLER and Dr. David Confer and the staffs of Saint Francis Hospital and Springer Clinic in Tulsa, Oklahoma, for saving my life from cancer in 1985. Secondly, to the wonderful people of my hometown of Tulsa, I thank you for reassuring me that I can always come home again.

This book would not be complete without mentioning the Reverend Richard Ziglar and his wife, Peggy, whose friendship toward my mother and me has created a lifelong bond. And I can't say enough about Tulsans Harvey and Carmen Dunham, who treated me like their own son when I was young.

To former KOTV Television General Manager Jim Moroney and current General Manager Ron Longinotti, who gave me a wonderful "welcome back" to Tulsa a few years ago, and my former colleagues Beth Rengal and Jim Giles, a heartfelt "thank you" for inviting me to cohost the Muscular Dystrophy Telethon.

To Dr. Joe Massad and his wife, Darlene, my eternal thanks for encouraging me to stick with this project.

This book wouldn't have happened at all without the driving force of *Tulsa People* Magazine Editor John Hamill. He was the first person to look at my original draft of the book and say, "I see some hope here." I've had high respect for John in the journalism field since he led the way while we were in high school.

Then there's Fred Ebrahimi. His advice on the book was invaluable. By the way, if you've got any complaints about the book, call Fred.

One guy who started me down the road to finishing this project was my friend for over thirty years, Jim Doran. His book on musician Erroll Garner is still considered the definitive work on Garner's fascinating life.

To my mentor in journalism, Mrs. Sheila Parr: You changed my life! You took a skinny little guy searching for a career and gave him a reason to succeed.

Much gratitude to Jack English, who first suggested I write this book, and to author and humorist Bo Whaley, who introduced me to Hillsboro Press.

To Andy, Mary Bray, Debbie, Marilyn, Lacie, Gary, Elaine, Holly, Stephen, Max, Darry, Charles, and Michael, the outstanding crew at Providence House Publishers and Hillsboro Press, who put their hearts and souls into designing the cover, researching, editing, and spreading the good news about the book. You've made me a very grateful author.

Finally, this book would not be complete without thanking my mother from the bottom of my heart. She's always been there for me, always loved me, and always put me ahead of herself. *Mom, you're loved more than words can say.*

Introduction

THIS IS THE CITY . . . ATLANTA, GEORGIA, . . . HOME OF CNN.

The stories you are about to read are true.

The names, when I've felt a little mercy, have been deleted to protect the innocent.

My name is Losure.

I carry a resume.

("Dragnet" theme music, please.)

September 7, 1994. I was working another weekend anchor shift at Headline News. In between the numbing stories of crime—stabbings, shootings, natural disasters, I made a decision—I had seen enough mayhem. It was time for a little sunshine.

The next day I put on my best suit and my brightest CNN smile and headed to a local church for the wedding of a Headline News coworker.

I didn't know many people in the wedding party. At the conclusion of a beautiful ceremony, I confidently walked up to the first fellow in the reception line and saw that he was grinning from ear to ear. I leaned over and extended my hand, glad that someone had recognized me.

Sure enough he did.

"Hey, Chuck Roberts! I've been wanting to meet you, doggone it! I watch you every afternoon!"

I paused. I looked over my shoulder. No, there was no Chuck Roberts behind me. I turned back around. The fellow whispered something to his wife and turned back to face me.

"Honey, I want you to meet Chuck Roberts from CNN. Gosh, it's good to meet a guy I grew up watching!"

I didn't have the heart to correct him. By now, his wife's hand was extended in my direction. I reached out with mine.

"It's a pleasure, ma'am. I'm Chuck. Chuck Roberts."

Then the third person in line reacted. She held out a pen and the wedding program. Suddenly, I was becoming a one-man PR team for my esteemed colleague, Chuck Roberts.

"Oh, you want an autograph?" I inquired. "Well heck, just give me that wedding program and old Chuck will sign it."

By now I was getting kind of used to my new identity. I then began to think of how far I could go with all this. Maybe I could even be somebody else. Maybe, let's see . . . Larry King?

As I smiled in self-satisfaction, the thought occurred to me that everyone might be going along with my little charade just to avoid telling me to my face what a poor sense of humor I had.

I signed the wedding program and raised my head to look down the reception line. My knees nearly buckled. I had fourteen more people to go. . . .

Actually, to be truthful, I learned a valuable lesson at that wedding. No matter who you think you are, someone will correct you.

In this book, I've probably spent an average of six hours per page trying to get it right. In many pages, you may conclude that I wasted five hours and thirty minutes, and probably did as well as I was going to do in the first half-hour. I have tried to condense thirty years in broadcasting into a book that will inform and entertain you.

Perhaps in some small way, I can reach out to some of you who have had cancer, or are going through it today. I have had a taste of what you're dealing with, and I hope by sharing my story, you'll find hope.

I also want to encourage reporters and anchors to fulfill their dreams. There's an exciting world out there for journalists, and a great deal of satisfaction available to those who will stick with it.

So stand by, the news is about to begin.

CHAPTER ONE

CNN's Finest Hour

IT WAS EARLY EVENING, JANUARY 16, 1991. ATLANTA. THE CNN newsroom and Headline News two floors below it were just receiving word that antiaircraft fire had been heard across the city of Baghdad. Were the Iraqi gunners test firing their antiaircraft weapons, or had the much-anticipated U.S. air strikes begun?

CNN correspondents John Holliman, Peter Arnett, and Bernie Shaw peered out the window of their Al-Rashid Hotel room in central Baghdad, watching the tracer rounds from Iraqi antiaircraft gunners make small, broken, orange lines in the air.

Within two minutes, the sound of loud explosions rumbled through downtown Baghdad.

Holliman was now sure the attack had begun and for the next several hours, only he and his colleagues would be the eyes and ears for a world eagerly hanging on every word of these three brave men.

CNN had worked hard for months to wield its considerable international influence to get Saddam Hussein to allow a four-wire phone system to be installed in the Al-Rashid. It meant that if power went off to the hotel, CNN would have its own generators to stay on the air by satellite. Permission for the four-wire system was granted just in time, because as other networks went off the air as the bombing started that night, CNN bypassed the hotel's dead phone system and put its mark on history.

Both anchor David Goodnow and I stood at the Headline News supervisor's desk shifting our attention from one TV monitor to another when the air raid began. Suddenly ABC's Gary Sheppard was cut off in midsentence as ABC lost its signal to the outside world. The attack had begun, and CNN was the only network on the air by satellite from Baghdad.

Lynne Russell was anchoring her 7:00 P.M. to 11:00 P.M. shift on Headline News—or "Headlines" as we call it—and was handed the long-awaited bulletin. Goodnow sat down at the update desk set in the newsroom just thirty-five feet from Russell's anchor desk. Within minutes he began giving the latest details. At 11 P.M. Russell ended her shift and Goodnow moved to her anchor chair. I moved to the update desk.

Producers and writers were suddenly violating a long-standing policy at Headline News, and no one was worried about it: Instead of sending messages by computer, they were *shouting* facts across the newsroom. We hurriedly took CNN's nighttime video of the antiaircraft fire and explosions, re-cued the video, and let the dramatic words of Holliman, Shaw, and Arnett tell the story.

Unsubstantiated reports were coming in from every TV network. If you had given me a test fifteen minutes after I broadcast some of the bulletins, I would not have been able to tell you what I had just said. New facts were pouring in that fast.

With little information from the Pentagon, and with hundreds of air strikes still in progress, we muddled our way through by repeating the same few facts over and over. While the obvious drama was in the live television accounts of eyewitnesses as explosions thundered around them, there was another drama being played out on the roughly seventy radio stations around the country who carry the Headline News audio, and it must have seemed like Orson Welles's "The War of the Worlds" broadcast again. Welles's radio broadcast in the 1930s, dramatizing an invasion of New Jersey by space aliens, was so real that tens of thousands panicked. Now, here again was this rather surreal event, with reporters from CNN in the midst of the bombing, just as CBS legend Edward R. Murrow and his colleagues had been during live broadcasts from London during the German bombings of that city in World War II.

Holliman, Arnett, and Shaw continued their vivid descriptions into a second hour. Huddled in their now-darkened hotel room in Baghdad, they continued their nonstop stream of information, punctuated by ear-deafening blasts as the U.S. Tomahawk cruise missiles from the ships, and the air-to-ground missiles and smart bombs hit their targets as close as two hundred yards away. Incredibly, the signal coming from that Baghdad hotel room was not cut off for nearly eight hours. They had played a cat-and-mouse game with the Iraqi guards at the Al-Rashid, putting their equipment under the beds and pretending to be asleep as the guards approached to check their room, then hooking the gear up immediately after the guards' departure. In fact, Bernie Shaw wasn't supposed to be there at all. He had come to get an interview with Saddam Hussein, then found that with the air strike looming, there was no time to get out of Baghdad.

The morning of January 17 dawned in Baghdad and Allied forces were back at their bases, re-arming for what would be another night of bombing runs. Back at the CNN Center in Atlanta, it was one in the morning, and there was still an immense amount of work to be done to edit the tremendous amount of tape that had poured in by satellite from not only Baghdad, but the staging areas in Dhahran, Saudi Arabia, where planes were being re-armed, and from aircraft carriers and guided-missile cruisers from which many of the F/A-18 and F-14 attack aircraft and Tomahawk cruise missiles had come. But there was hardly time to catch a breath.

By early evening, Saddam Hussein was trying to get revenge. More information from sources in Jerusalem, Haifa, and Tel Aviv were flooding CNN and Headline News two floors below with more data than we could get on the air.

The activity suddenly focused on deadly Scud missile attacks on Israel. I was at the update desk at Headline News, trying to listen to a dozen people around me even as words were being spoken into my ear by the producer in the director's booth. The movie "Broadcast News," with its anchors being given their information just in time for them to repeat it, was coming to life.

Headline News, 7:49 P.M., January 17: "This is Bob Losure at the CNN Headline News Update desk. Pentagon sources say Tel

Aviv, Israel, is now under a Scud missile attack from Iraq. At least five missiles reportedly have been launched. Apparently three have hit. NBC news is reporting one of them carried chemical weapons. Apparently several explosions were heard across the city of Tel Aviv. Again, no missiles have hit Jerusalem. . . . We now have reports from Dhahran, Saudi Arabia, that reporters and guests at hotels are being evacuated to air raid shelters. The civil defense feels missiles could be incoming there. More in 10 minutes. . . . "

Headline News, 7:53 P.M.: "The U.S.-led air assault on Iraq is pounding targets in Kuwait. A CNN correspondent describing the scene in Kuwait says B-52s are carpet-bombing Iraqi positions . . . meanwhile hundreds of Iraqi casualties, victims of the underground resistance movement in Kuwait are being reported in Kuwait City . . . sources at the Pentagon say U.S.-led allied air attacks have been 80 percent effective on Iraqi targets. Sources say no allied troops have crossed into Kuwait, but a source says a lot of U.S. ground forces are moving toward the Kuwaiti border. Baghdad radio claims sixty Allied planes have been shot down. Saddam Hussein said President Bush is the 'Satan in the White House.' As Hussein put it, 'The victory is assured, God willing.'"

Headline News 8:01 P.M.: "Missiles from Iraq were launched against Israel this evening. Three have hit Tel Aviv. One target that was hit was a hospital. Two have hit in Haifa, Israel, as well as one in Sproch, Israel. NBC is reporting that one hospital is reportedly taking care of chemical weapons victims. Apparently one of the missiles carried chemical weapons. Jerusalem has not been hit. Twelve to thirteen missiles have been heard. You can see that correspondent Larry Register has his gas mask on in Jerusalem. We now go to Richard Roth, live in Tel Aviv with more there:

'Right now, I'm on the sixth floor of the Hilton, in a sealed room with dozens of other reporters. We've heard ten or eleven explosions—it's unclear what kind—reverberating throughout the city. Sometime around 2:15 in the morning local time, the air raid sirens went off, and this city, which had been bracing for several weeks for potential trouble, raced into sealed rooms, and donned gas masks. I'm sitting next to dozens of people who are wearing their black gas masks. People are being told to stay put. No smoking.

We are not able to look outside because we're sealed off. We just keep hearing loud explosions and booms going off. Some people thought the worst might be over and Saddam Hussein might not be able to fulfill his threats. Apparently, that might have been wishful thinking.'"

Headline News, 8:03 P.M.: "The Pentagon is now reporting that at least eight missiles have been launched toward Israel. As you'll be hearing from our correspondents, Israel has said it would strike back if Iraq attacked it. The Pentagon says Israel will be responding. Pilots have been sitting in their planes on Israeli runways on a twenty-four-hour-a-day basis for the past three days. It now appears Israeli bombers and fighters are preparing to take off to retaliate at any moment. Now, here's Lou Dobbs, who has a report from Larry Register, our bureau chief in Jerusalem:

'Lou, we're looking over the Knesset building in Jerusalem from our bureau window. I'm looking up into the skies. There's a bit of panic here right now. We're trying to get in contact with our bureau in Tel Aviv, but we haven't been able to reach them.'"

Headline News, 8:07 P.M.: "American military sources are giving more details about last night's onslaught against the Iraqis. They say Iraqi radar, telephone, and active Scud missile sites have been knocked out. They also say that the bombing created craters on Iraqi runways. Fifty percent of Iraq's airport has been destroyed. Four Allied aircraft have been lost. They include two British Tornados, one Kuwaiti aircraft, and one American F/A-18. The pilot of the F/A-18 reportedly died. NBC news is reporting that nerve gas from Scud missiles has been dropped on Tel Aviv. Victims have been taken to hospitals."

The nonstop pace continued for another three nights, as U.S. Tomahawk cruise missiles found their mark, and more American air sorties did their work, getting ever closer to Saddam Hussein himself. Ten more days and the quick, decisive ground campaign had made short work of the war. Little did CNN know that it had created a world of insomniacs, with many viewers waiting for that next big war to be televised. . . .

Most of us at Headline News never felt we would see such an event again in our lifetimes . . . but there it was, the end of 1997, and Peter Arnett, Brent Sadler, and Ben Wedemen were at the Al-Rashid Hotel, with more saber rattling by Saddam Hussein in the face of another American buildup of forces in the Persian Gulf.

Just as the American military had come up with more technological advantages over Saddam Hussein with the B-1 bomber and stealth technology, CNN had also upped its technology level. Better nightscope cameras were in place to give a less-grainy picture of any nighttime bombing of Baghdad. Preparations were in place for clearer satellite feeds of CNN reports.

Saddam Hussein seemed to be relishing the chance to get CNN reporters and their camera crews to any scene where there might be civilian casualties among the "human shields" that he had allegedly recruited to camp next to his defense installations and his many palaces. Fortunately Saddam blinked first in the game of brinkmanship with the U.S military at the end of 1997, but he likely will test the patience of United Nations weapons inspectors for years.

I'm asked frequently why reporters and technical crews from CNN would want to stay in harm's way by remaining in Baghdad. The truth is that many of us who have spent time covering violence and massive tragedy as journalists generally have an innate desire to be in the middle of the excitement, no matter how dangerous, and eager to be the first ones to report on a big story. In many cases, CNN journalists and technical support people remain today in precarious, life-threatening situations not just in Baghdad, but Bosnia as well as many African countries. The sniper who nearly killed CNN photographer Margaret Moth while she was riding in a car to the Sarajevo airport a few years ago is testament to the dangers. Yet many CNN journalists stay in these out-of-the-way powder kegs month in and month out not for the glory, or the combat pay, but for a little higher calling . . . to probe, and then probe some more to seek out the truth.

Sometimes that truth is almost impossible to get at. CNN and other network reporters thought they had the problem solved for getting through the military maze and red tape to report from the front lines, after being kept well away from the fighting in the U.S. invasion of Panama a few years ago. Yet the problem resurfaced in the Persian Gulf War, with reporters held back from being able to see what the U.S. military was doing. Would Americans know if Iraqi prisoners were massacred? Would families back home have any idea of how the destruction of nerve gas and biological agents was being done? Were friendly-fire deaths greater than actually reported?

The significance of inflated body counts of dead North Vietnamese soldiers in Vietnam, the extent of the presidential coverup of the Watergate break-in, and the obvious inconsistencies in the investigation of the Kennedy assassination were glossed over for months, even years, and the media felt it had been duped in each instance. Those three events alone have triggered much of the media's negativity and hostility toward authority of any kind, and that in turn has filtered down to the way many of our young people distrust society today.

The American public is the loser when its eyes and ears, namely the U.S. media, are arbitrarily excluded from knowing what their government and armed forces are doing. The day will come, as it did at the My Lai massacre in Vietnam in the 1960s, when Americans will find out—all too late—the real truth. Unless Americans demand that the rules for government cooperation with the media on stories like the invasion of Panama and the front lines of the Persian Gulf War are changed, the chances for trust in our government will diminish.

I want to close this chapter with a little positive news—the immeasurable effect of instant global news coverage. I was in Prague, Czechoslovakia, in 1989 when the revolution from college students and veteran antiwar activists helped continue the domino effect that had crumbled totalitarian governments from Poland to East Berlin, and from Estonia to Lithuania. It makes me proud for those who carry the banner of CNN and other news organizations into threatening situations in war zones like the Middle East each and every day.

Just as there are fearless reporters and photographers, electronic signals also have no fear. They cross borders without leaving a single casualty. Even governments have a hard time keeping up with the proliferation of satellite dishes around the world. Satellite technology, coupled with global signals from CNN and CNN International, spread the reality of what freedom and free enterprise are all about. As Ted Turner has pointed out, some people in the third world can in the late 1990s finally receive the same news we're dispensing in the first world.

Satellite downlinks, carrying the CNN Havana bureau's stories of increasing poverty in Cuba, are rapidly setting that country on a new course toward freedom. Slowly, perhaps painfully so, Iraqis are finding out through the lens of the camera what their government has done to its own people.

In a far less brutal, but equally dramatic scene, Americans were educated in 1968 as they watched the Democratic National Convention. News reports for the first time were showing live pictures of the brutality in the streets of Chicago. Dozens of cameras captured the truth that night, and the chant from the protesters, "The whole world is watching! The whole world is watching!" was prophetic. Thirty years later, the American media has the tools to do its job in time of peace and in time of crisis, but it is only the American public, armed with knowledge, who can decide how truly free the media remains from government interference. Perhaps CNN's finest hour is still to come. Today, the whole world really is watching.

CHAPTER TWO

A Day in the Life of . . .

I'VE OFTEN BEEN ASKED WHAT IT WAS LIKE TO BE IN THE middle of an anchor shift and suddenly have to read an exciting bulletin on the air . . . perhaps ad-libbing some background on the story, and maybe not even disclosing all the facts for fear it would be too provocative or too gruesome for the audience to handle.

First of all, I *never, ever* hid the truth no matter how gruesome the story was. We would, however, hold back on unsubstantiated facts until they could be corroborated by reliable sources.

Secondly, despite the giant reach of thousands of newspaper and wire service reporters around the world, bulletins of something really important didn't occur every day. Of course, since I was anchoring Saturday or Sunday night, doing a double shift of eight hours on the air each night till 3:00 A.M., I was always hoping for a bulletin just to break the monotony.

The excitement of sitting in the anchor chair and delivering one bulletin after another during the air and ground campaign of the Persian Gulf War may never be matched again . . . at least until the next war somewhere in the world. So my typical Saturday or Sunday routine prior to going on the air at 7:00 P.M. was not geared for excitement.

I began by opening a can of tennis balls at approximately 1:00 P.M. All right, I'll speed it up here. Frequently I would play tennis with my good friend Gene Godefroid, a forty-five-year-old Equifax programmer who must work out twenty-three hours a day on his stationary bike. He runs down every ball I hit into his court, then slashes it back at near-warp speed. I have dubbed him *Gene-Gene, The Tennis Machine*, and I've learned to accept defeat gracefully . . . since I've gotten a lot of practice at it.

After limping off the tennis court, I showered, put some black jeans on along with a dress shirt, picked out a tie, got a suit coat from the closet, and then grabbed a pair of white socks.

I know what you're thinking. What is he going to wear with white socks? Tennis shoes, of course. No, not the ones I had just played in, but another pair, guaranteed to make me feel just a little like a rebel on a Saturday night, but also practical enough to be good to my feet.

Then I grabbed my makeup kit and examined it for all the necessary items: No-Name makeup (it's made in New York, and that really is the name), contacts, contact solution, hair brush, and IFB cord (that's the interrupted feedback device which I wore in my right ear to hear the producer).

Those items would be all that the normal male anchor would need to take. Of course, as you will see, I may not be normal. The words *disorganized* and *seldom punctual* come to mind, though I never missed getting to work on time. I would come so close that anchor Judy Fortin and the Headline News crew must have thought I was trying to give them a heart attack.

What I also brought with me in that makeup kit were several Alka-Seltzers, some Tylenol and Advil, cough drops, change for the candy machine, solution in case my eyes turned red, extra pens, a tiny sewing kit, and a small mirror (just in case the one at the anchor desk *breaks* when I see my reflection). I used all those items during my career at Headline News. My father had always been the kind of guy who prepared for whatever small things might be needed. He must have been a Boy Scout, and I followed his supreme example of preparedness.

I left my apartment about 5:00 P.M. for the O-K Cafe, a twenty-four-hour Atlanta institution with food just like Mom used to make—pot roast, chicken pot pie, meat loaf—and served up by a great bunch of people. They were and are my listening post for what people think about the news. I was kind of like Norm from the television show "Cheers," perched on the same stool at the counter every day I came in.

By 6:00 P.M. I was on my way to the CNN Center in downtown Atlanta, daring the weather and potential traffic snarls to make me late. In fact, that 6:00 P.M. departure time for the fifteen-minute drive downtown was on a *good* day. There were numerous times when I screeched to a halt in the CNN parking lot, raced across the pedestrian skyway into the CNN Center, down the steps, past the security checkpoint, into the Headline News reception area, then right past Judy Fortin at the anchor desk, on my way to the men's room.

Opening my makeup kit, I placed one contact in the left eye so I could see the teleprompter at a distance. The right eye didn't need one since it was for reading the paper script in my hand. (Believe it or not, it can be done successfully.)

Then with two drops of water on my makeup sponge, I whisked the sponge across the pressed powder three or four times, then applied it with short, even strokes across my forehead, into the hairline, down my nose, across the ears, down the cheeks, the chin, and finally under my nose. The motion was probably similar to a brick mason using a trowel, but for some strange reason it worked.

Next, I pulled the four-foot-long IFB cord and earpiece out of my makeup kit, one end of which went down the back side under my coat, then under my belt, to be plugged into a receptacle on the side of the anchor desk. I pulled the other end of the cord up over the back of my neck and placed the molded earpiece snugly in my ear.

I ran my hairbrush through my hair half-a-dozen times, straightened my tie, brushed the lint off my coat lapel, and presto! The instant anchorman in less than four minutes!

I know you must be wondering why I was such a procrastinator that I ended up in this frenzy at the last second. Instead of trying to be my own form of Superman, able to leap tall mounds of news copy at a single bound, why didn't I plan ahead and go to a CNN makeup artist upstairs?

I have no excuse. Even this book took two years to write. Maybe I was a *rebel anchor without a cause*. It wasn't that I put off sitting in the anchor chair for fear of the eight-hour shift ahead. I think I had and still have a natural trait for seeing how close I can cut it, thereby getting my adrenaline working at full speed.

So, in those final ninety seconds before air, I'd look at the hand-held mirror in mock terror, try to get my tie somewhere close to centered, my cowlick pressed back down, and the shine on my nose buffed one more time.

Then I plugged in the IFB cord, turned the volume knob just short of an ear-piercing setting, and almost immediately was asked for a check of the microphone volume from the director's booth.

"Never attempt to wrestle a pig. You'll both get dirty, and only the pig will enjoy it," I'd blurt out. I could almost hear the collective, depressing sigh in the director's booth as I used that idiotic phrase for the ten-thousandth time.

By then it was 6:59 P.M., and the producer in the director's booth was talking to me through the IFB. "Can you hear me?"

Naturally I'd throw up my hands in mock confusion as the hapless and now panic-stricken producer repeated the question only to see me on their monitor doing the same expression again.

Then those words from the cameraperson that actually caught my attention—"Thirty seconds to air, Bob."

I was a million miles away mentally, trying to recall who that former anchor was who once pronounced the name of that little breed of dogs, Chihuahua, as "Chuh-who-uh-who-uh." "Fifteen seconds, Bob."

Then there was the anchor who called Jimmy Buffet "Jimmy Buf-fay." "Five seconds, Bob."

And that anchor whose colleagues on the anchor set nearly doubled over in laughter when he called the Hong Kong Flu the "King Kong Flu."

"STAND BY BOB! WE'RE IN THE OPEN!"

(Announcer:) "Live, from the CNN Center . . ."

(Cameraperson cues Bob)

(Bob:) "Good evening, at the top of the news at this hour, seven members of a vacationing family drowned Saturday night in the same lake where Susan Smith drowned her two children. . . ."

As the rapid-fire pace continued and I introduced fifteen-second soundbites and reporter's stories, I was scrambling to read ahead as far as I could while listening to the producer talk to me about stories that were to be eliminated for time considerations.

In the first hour, writers and editors were frantically trying to get a mountain of news copy to me just seconds before I delivered it to the audience on the air. Sometimes I didn't even get the copy in my hand, but had to explore the world of kamikaze broadcasting—reading whatever was on the prompter.

One thing I couldn't fake was pronouncing all those strange names. Slobodan Milosevic. Alija Itzebegovic. Ratko Mladic. Yes, they were real human beings, not Ukrainian dinner entrées.

That's where the electronic prompter helped immensely. An electronic prompter, which Headline News began using in 1994, has the copy electronically generated as either black against a white background, or white against a black background, and the words are far easier to read than the old system of individual pages gliding on a conveyor belt beneath an overhead camera that then displays the copy across the two-way mirror on the front of the camera.

The old system, used for forty years in many stations, was only as good as the lighting on the conveyor belt and the quick reflexes of the operator to keep the pages from curling up under each other. Some nights at Headline News fingernails and knuckles appeared across the teleprompter copy as the operator reached in to keep the pages straight on the conveyor belt.

Reading from a little fourteen-by-fourteen-inch screen about fifteen feet away is a specialized art, especially when you're five or six hours into an eight-hour doubleshift. By then I was earning my pay not just for keeping my tongue and jaw working in harmony, but for staying attentive like an air traffic controller, waiting for that moment known as a *technical difficulty.*

When it happened, the key was to never let the audience see you sweat. I might be looking down at the monitor on the anchor desk for ten seconds (which can seem like eternity), waiting for a report to play, or for the director or producer to give me some guidance. Eventually I'd be told what to do through my IFB, hopefully in calming, soothing tones, and not a frantic overmodulation that would sound like a firecracker going off in my head.

"We're apparently having some technical difficulties," I'd tell the audience. "We'll get back to that story a little later on."

Those were the easy kinds of flubs. There were times when our own train wreck would occur, and all we could do was damage control.

One night a few years before we switched to the electronic prompter, I started reading a page that the prompter operator had placed in the wrong order.

"Bob, you're on the wrong page," shouted the producer in my ear. "When you finish page nine, go back to page seven."

I looked down. There was not a page seven to be found in my copy. I looked at the prompter operator, then back at the camera.

"Pardon me for a moment," I deadpanned.

I pressed down on the "cough" button to mute my microphone, turned to the prompter operator and said "If you've got page seven, load it up, then follow it with page ten."

The prompter operator looked back in stark terror. She had never seen an anchor talk to her while they were on the air.

Then I opened my mouth to speak again, hoping that there were no lip readers in the audience, since the camera was still on me. There was no time to call a staff meeting and ask for a vote on what to do. "Did you hear what I said?"

The prompter operator scurried through her pile of copy. Then I waited. Time was marching on. Page seven suddenly appeared in the prompter. I let go of the cough button, thanked the audience for their indulgence, and began reading page seven.

On a normal night, the problems never reached that scale. The biggest decision might be how to get to the bathroom and back without bringing the show to a halt.

The first rule to observe if you know you're going to be sitting in a chair for two hours and thirteen minutes without getting up is this: *Never have chili before going to work.* From 7:00 P.M. to 9:13 P.M. I only had three and a half minutes during the sports report at :20 and :50 past the hour. Many nights I looked forward to *sports*.

The major problem was staying focused on what I was doing for eight hours. I did what are called cut-ins, or thirteen-minute news segments at 9:00, 9:30, 10:00, and 10:30 P.M., allowing me some breaks that were a bit longer.

During the second two hours of each four-hour shift, the master control director would replay part of what I'd done in my first two hours. So I was in the seat for about six hours each Saturday and Sunday night.

If we made a mistake in those first two hours, then we had to redo it when the mistake came up in the replay in the final two hours. So I might be called back to sit at the anchor set at 10:24 P.M., wait for a soundbite to play from the master tape, then jump in live and read up until the next soundbite or reporter's piece played on the tape. It was amazing to me how the engineering geniuses had figured out how to go from the master tape to me live, then back to the re-cued tape without a break in the action.

Every now and then, maybe just once a year, we would try to correct a mistake on the replay, and the unthinkable would happen. The sound portion replayed from the master tape but for a reason known only to a trained engineer, the video did not. It meant I had to lip synch the words and follow along just as if I were speaking to them, kind of like a rock group feels when it's lip-synching a record in a *live* performance and the music stops.

I've often been asked if I ever said a dirty word on the air, or was caught scratching my nose, combing my hair, or worse. *I never did.* I came very, very close numerous times, but I treated the microphone as if it were always open. I also seemed to feel when a camera was about to be switched on. When I was combing my hair on the anchor set, both the hand and the comb disappeared out of camera range in the split second it took for the TV picture to change from a report to me.

Even with the so-called *bump shots*, where a third camera was positioned to get a wide shot of the entire set, my tennis shoes only showed up on camera two or three times. It got to the point where I felt like I wanted to be part of a blooper tape, but I just didn't have the right stuff.

By the time 3:00 A.M. came, I was tired, but still too "up" from charging through the copy at 185 words a minute to slow down all at once. So I'd stop on the way home at, where else, the O-K Cafe, eat a cheeseburger with a side of onion rings, and drive on home.

Any doctor will tell you that's the healthiest thing you can do.

CHAPTER THREE

Getting My Kicks on Route 66

MY FATHER, HOMER LOSURE, WAS A DISCIPLINARIAN, but he also showed me a lot of good times—fishing trips to a lake near Tulsa, Oklahoma, and vacations back to his midwestern roots in the farming community of Van Buren, Indiana.

Dad suffered from emphysema caused by smoking three packs of cigarettes a day for forty years. He took early retirement from Gulf Oil Corporation after serving thirty-five years there as an accountant. He died in 1975 of a self-inflicted gunshot wound. He had gasped for air for years, even when he walked the short distance from the house to the car. At 112 pounds, he finally tired of the struggle.

My mother, Larama Losure, is a study in courage, perseverance, and caring. She walks on legs bolstered inside by titanium braces. She's like a fighter who gets knocked down ten times in a fight, and still answers the bell for the tenth round. She's broken some ribs, her right shoulder, her left wrist, and both legs in the last five years, but she's still moving with courage down the road of life.

I fly in from Atlanta once a month to visit her at Heatheridge Assisted Living Center, and we make the Piccadilly Cafeteria and TCBY Yogurt our mandatory stops. In her case, there are advantages to weighing just eighty pounds. You can get two scoops of ice cream and not feel guilty. I, on the other hand, shouldn't even be allowed through the front door.

Little Bobby and his proud
parents, 1950.

My mother was raised in Westfork and Fort Smith, Arkansas,
and came to Tulsa to work as a secretary. She and my father met on
a blind date in 1946, married in September of that year, and I
arrived in this world as their first and only child on May 4, 1947.

From the time I was old enough to go on a trip, my parents took
me to Spavinaw Lake, seventy miles northeast of Tulsa. I loved the
outdoors and all the animals that inhabited the woods. To be able
to have a cabin, even one that was borrowed, was a dream come
true. Like a Norman Rockwell painting, the orange-colored lights
in the houses a hundred yards below our cabin at night cast a glow
into the woods, and the smell of the burning oak, wafting from the
chimneys, was unforgettable.

To this day, I can remember the thrill of scurrying after lizards
as they darted around the rocks. There was also the taste of hot,
steaming homemade stew being dished up. Then at night when I
got in bed, I was still riding the waves in our fishing boat. As my
head lay back on the pillow, I was asleep in less than a minute,
dreaming of reeling in the bass and bluegill, one after another.

One of my earliest memories of Tulsa was the sound of cars at
night, traveling in an almost endless procession on Route 66, that
historic highway that went from Chicago to Los Angeles. We lived
about fifty yards from Route 66, near Eleventh and Cheyenne in
downtown Tulsa.

Since we had no air-conditioning and few fans, we slept in the
middle of the backyard on army cots under mosquito netting draped
across poles for part of the summer. To me, it was just another form

Yours truly, age four.

of camping out, and in those days the only thing you might worry about was the occasional rainstorm or a 'possum crossing the yard in the middle of the night on his way to dine at a neighbor's trash can.

I was seven years old in late 1954 when I saw my first television star in person, appearing at a local department store.

It was Davy Crockett in the flesh, complete with his coonskin cap—Actor Fess Parker, all six feet, five inches of him, was towering over me, casting a huge shadow, and extending his hand to me and my mother. He made King Kong look small. *I don't think I washed my right hand for a week.*

The "Lone Ranger" theme was moved to the back shelf. The "Ballad of the Alamo" became a permanent fixture on my little record player, whirling around at 78 rpms.

Soon, my twin bed was covered with a Davy Crockett bedspread. My trip to the bathroom in the middle of the night was lighted by the trusty beam of my Davy Crockett flashlight.

Christmas came and I was seated squarely in front of the black-and-white TV, adjusting the rabbit ears to see Davy and Jim Bowie swinging their muskets at General Santa Ana's men from the ramparts of the Alamo. Walt Disney had me right where he wanted me.

A year later we moved to a new area of Tulsa known as Brookside. I was small and skinny, afraid of the loud noise of fireworks, but never afraid of walking across a four-foot-wide sewer pipe across an inlet to try to catch fish at the nearby Arkansas River.

My good friend Rick Dunham, who spent a lot of days sitting out there on that pipe with me, remembers that we could only be lured back home by one thing: food. We had mothers who knew what it took to get us back home.

My mother was also quite a collector of photographs, too. In fact she had lots of pictures in scrapbooks showing me from the time I was just old enough to walk, sitting there naked in the bathtub, naked on a picnic blanket, and naked in my stroller. She was also eager to share her precious photos with anyone who would look. Years later she shared them with a film crew, and they shared them with half of the city of Tulsa.

It happened in 1992 when I was honored along with two others with a Distinguished Alumni Award from my alma mater, the University of Tulsa. Much to my embarrassment, and much to the delight of an audience of over eight hundred, those same naked baby pictures of me were blown up to the size of Godzilla, and paraded in agonizingly slow-motion across a twelve-by-fifteen-foot screen.

As I approached the podium to accept my award, the laughter began to build from the audience.

"Ladies and gentlemen," I began, "I believe you will agree with me that after the risqué pictures you have seen displayed this evening, it will be only fitting that I remove the word 'distinguished' from this beautiful plaque. . . ."

The audience responded with laughter, and my eighty-three-year-old mom was laughing the loudest. . . .

An embarassing baby photo. Courtesy of Mom.

Exposure by Losure

BACK IN THE SEVENTH GRADE IN JUNIOR HIGH SCHOOl, I rode my bicycle about six miles to the downtown Tulsa library, checking out books like *The Hound of the Baskervilles* and *Journey to the Center of the Earth*.

Then at the school library I began to explore everything from *Great Expectations* to *Huckleberry Finn* to *A Connecticut Yankee in King Arthur's Court*. I liked to get lost in imagining what the characters looked like, and what it would be like to travel from one time period to another, and one country to another.

In the spring of 1963, my sophomore year at Edison High School in Tulsa, all that reading finally began to pay off. My English teacher, Sheila Parr, changed my life with a simple question:

"Bob, how about joining my journalism class this fall?"

Journalism? Me, a newspaper writer? The closest I had come to writing was a book report on some of my favorite authors like Sir Arthur Conan Doyle, Mark Twain, Charles Dickens, and H. G. Wells.

Suddenly I realized that I might actually become *somebody*. Not just an average student at a high school that had graduated dozens of National Merit Scholarship semifinalists. I could write about the Thespian Club, or the rules for putting combination locks on your locker, and my high school classmates would have no choice but to read it, perhaps with my byline at the top!

My senior year I was editor of the school paper and writer or advertising salesman for just about every other paper in town. I even had my own column: "Exposure by Losure." Of course I didn't *expose* anything, except maybe my ignorance. In those days, 1963–1965, in Tulsa, I didn't even think of writing anything remotely controversial.

There was only one problem with all this journalistic work: I didn't have a car to do the paying job, covering sports for the *Tulsa World*. Come to think of it, I didn't have a license either . . . since I had flunked the driving exam three times.

The first time, I ran a stop sign. Second time, I went the wrong way on a one-way street. The third time, I made a left turn in front of an oncoming car at the crest of a hill, nearly causing the driving test officer to have a heart attack.

My driver's education teachers denied knowing me.

However, I had Plan B to get around all that. I enlisted the help of my high school buddy, John Hetherington, who, with no social life himself, was going to be my chauffeur. He too, could be dangerous behind the wheel of his '50 Ford, but at least he did have a license.

My most memorable event as a young reporter was a high school basketball game one night on the west side of Tulsa. My high school, the Edison Eagles, beat the Webster Warriors in Webster's gym. Simple enough.

John hauled me back to the *Tulsa World* building so I could get the story in the morning edition.

However, as I sat at my typewriter, things weren't adding up. I knew Edison High School won, but the score I added up showed Webster *winning*. Then, the more I thought about it, the more uncertain I became.

This was starting to look like a dilemma. I couldn't call up one of the coaches and say, "Hey, I'm *Tulsa World* reporter Bob Losure. Could you tell me who won the game that I covered tonight?"

Finally, I called John, we piled in the Ford, and took off for Webster's gym. I jumped out in a panic and banged on the door of the gym until the janitor answered. I rather sheepishly explained who I was, and asked if he would please turn on the scoreboard lights.

He did. Edison won 72 to 68.

For the first and let's hope the last time in my journalism career, I admit it—I fabricated some of the scores of the individual players to make it come out right.

There, I said it.

It took over thirty years to get that admission of guilt out of me . . . officially. I only made five bucks for covering the game, too.

To my journalism teacher, Mrs. Parr, who was such a great inspiration to me over the years, *I beg your forgiveness.*

Oh yes, there's a very small story I almost left out about my social life in high school. You see, I had no social life. My first date was when I was almost seventeen, in the spring of my junior year, 1964. I went out with an older woman—a senior—whose name was Carol Cravens. I was so nervous on our double date that I shook hands with her at the end of the evening, I think.

I went out with perhaps half-a-dozen girls for the next year and a half until I graduated. The young ladies were beautiful and intelligent, but I still lacked the confidence to really relax and enjoy myself. So I stuck with what I knew best—writing.

CHAPTER FIVE

Mr. Losure
Goes to College

ONE OF THE ONLY GOOD THINGS ABOUT NOT HAVING many dates in high school is that you can channel your interest toward a career. My interest in journalism was strong enough that when I got turned down my junior year for the biggest prize out there—the five-week National High School Institute of Journalism at prestigious Northwestern University near Chicago—I was more determined than ever my senior year. Dreams do come true. I was accepted for the intensive five-week course for the summer following my senior year.

I was in journalism heaven—heaven on the shores of Lake Michigan.

I wrote stories from information yelled out at a rapid-fire pace by Northwestern University Professor Ben Baldwin. Those writing sessions were interspersed with trips to the *Chicago Tribune* and *Chicago Sun-Times* newspapers, Cubs and White Sox baseball games, and the College All-Stars working out at Soldier Field.

I really wanted to attend Northwestern in the fall of 1965, but I didn't have the money, and didn't get a scholarship. There was, however, a journalism scholarship available at the University of Oklahoma, and I was thankful to get it. My interest was still in newspaper reporting, but I was also fascinated by the thought of being a radio news announcer.

In high school I had watched play-by-play commentators from the local high school football games, and I thought it was exciting. So I transferred into a broadcast journalism curriculum my sophomore year.

Then the school made a big mistake—they let me go on the air.

One of my great friends then and now, Jim Doran, lived in my dorm at the University of Oklahoma. In addition to buying me more than a few submarine sandwiches at the nearby pizza joint called Dewey's, Jim also told me what I wanted to hear.

In other words, he could lie with the best of them.

He heard my first KUVY-FM student radio broadcast as the FM signal skipped across the South Oval, down some sidewalks, off a flag pole, and finally into the Cross Center dorms.

Jim told me I sounded like Edward R. Murrow.

My guess is that I sounded more like Mr. Ed, the talking horse on the TV show. I'm glad Jim hedged the truth a bit, because I was gullible enough to believe him and keep going with my broadcasting career.

Meanwhile, at the beginning of my sophomore year, my social life improved immeasurably . . . for about a month.

Her name was Susan Sullivan. We had gone out three or four times when one night, on a little footbridge over a place called the Duck Pond, Susan made the first move. She put her hands to the sides of my face, and laid one on me. *I thought I was in love.* At least the concept sounded real good to me at the time, and once the barrier crumbled, all I wanted to do was kiss that woman. She was cute, and so irresistible.

I even bought her a necklace and we were suddenly going steady, or "dropped" as it was called back then.

Two weeks later, she dropped me from her life.

I have come to realize over the years that a man and a woman in a romantic setting don't always have the same degree of attraction to each other for exactly the same period of time. Back then, however, I did not understand the mysterious ways of love. Susan had caught me, and she thought it was time to move on to the next catch.

I was devastated. I played the song "Cherish" endlessly on the turntable at the campus radio station for the next month. I played that record until I wore it out.

Then I moved on to a similarly deadly tune, given my condition, titled "Symphony for Susan," by the Arbors. I wore that record out, and eventually all the self-pity was wearing *me* out, along with my friends. It was time to get on with my life.

Even before the end of my sophomore year, I had missed my friends in Tulsa, so I returned to the University of Tulsa my junior year, becoming a member of Pi Kappa Alpha Fraternity, and making friends with guys that are still my friends over thirty years later. I spent the summer between my sophomore and junior years calling in baseball scores every three innings from the ballpark of the Tulsa triple-A baseball team, the Oilers. I had a great time, watching the guys in the press box call the play-by-play, gathering up a ten-year supply of baseballs that landed on the roof of the park, and dreaming of that first real broadcasting job at a commercial radio station that was bound to come my way soon.

There was a rather odd sign on the left field fence of the ballpark that read "To Sell 'Em, Tell 'Em! The Big Gun For Country Fun! KTOW, 1340 On Your Dial. Sand Springs, Oklahoma."

I thought, who would work in a place that played records by somebody named Skeeter Davis or Ferlin Husky? A pack of wild dogs would have to drag me, kicking and screaming, to get me into a place like that. . . .

Actually, there were no wild dogs involved. I simply walked into the studio.

A week after thinking about it, I swallowed my pride, and determined that since I couldn't start at the top in broadcasting, maybe I'd better go someplace where they might take pity on me. It was July 1967.

It was ironic that I had gone there to apply for a position in their news department, only to be informed by the station's program director that they had no news department. I was just about out the front door when the program director stopped me. He was starting up a midnight–5:00 A.M. disc jockey shift. It paid the giant sum of a dollar-sixty an hour . . . minimum wage.

I took it.

I fell asleep the first night on the air while playing the seven-minute version of Johnny Cash's "The Legend of John Henry's Hammer." My apologies to you, Johnny, if you read this, but those

Bob behind the microphone at Tulsa's KAKC radio in 1968, doing the 20/20 news format that was popular at the time.

long records could be killers if you were sleepy and it was the middle of the night.

At first I thought my tendency to fall asleep might be due to the fact that the records weren't any good. Then I discovered later how popular Johnny Cash, Loretta Lynn, Hank Williams, and Willie Nelson were. Of course, the fact that I was going to college during the day, doing my pledge duties in the evening at Pi Kappa Alpha Fraternity, and driving like a madman to get to Sand Springs late at night, may have had something to do with my enthusiasm.

My on-air name was now Country Bob Curtis. I figured the name Losure didn't sound very country, so I used my middle name. Across the street from the station, I discovered there were also some aliases being used. The upper floor of the two-story building was being used as a house of prostitution.

How did I know for sure? I had eyes, first of all, and some nights the participants forgot to draw the shades, perhaps in the interests of good advertising. I spent a lot of time at 2:00 and 3:00 A.M. climbing over the eight-foot wall of the program director's cubicle, (since I didn't have the key to his office) so I could get to the wall-sized window that faced the building.

I had my own little ringside seat for the show, and I gave it rave reviews, practicing my play by-play announcing and hoping that Johnny Cash's seven-minute record wouldn't run out before I scaled the wall back to the other side.

Twenty-seven years later, in 1994, the guy who trained me at KTOW, Bob Anderson, sent me the original record I had played my first night on the air: "Phantom 309" by Red Sovine. I know it was

When Air Force Captain Scott O'Grady flew into Atlanta in January of '96 and ask me over dinner if I'd like to say "hello" to the Beach Boys at the Georgia Dome, I had no idea we were going to literally "say hello to the Beach Boys."

the same record I had played back then, because it had some of my doodling on it.

Bob was typical of the folks I've met in country music over the years. They don't forget you, and he was very kind to remember me from his home in Muskagee, Oklahoma.

My eight months as an insomniac at KTOW was just enough, and in March 1968 I auditioned at KAKC Radio, then a popular rock-and-roll station. My demo tape was pitiful. KAKC program director Lee Bayley listened to about as much as he could stand of it, namely thirty seconds, hit the rewind button on the tape machine, put the tape back in its box, and sent me on my way.

I left like a dog with his tail hanging between his legs, dropping my résumé on the floor as I left.

Bayley picked it up, probably to put it in the trash can. He must have glanced at the news experience I had, because a week later he called and hired me for what I actually wanted to do—news.

That job turned into the most fun I've ever had in my career. It didn't pay much, but I got to listen to some great rock-and-roll: The Doors, Marvin Gaye, Jefferson Airplane, and the Beach Boys. Being a serious newscaster would have to wait.

The DJs were also guys I had idolized since high school. If I could have changed careers in those formative years in my early twenties, I would either have tried to be a play-by-play sports announcer or a disc jockey. In retrospect, I think I picked the right career for me.

CHAPTER SIX

The Motor City and Byron MacGregor

IN MAY OF 1969 I WAS ABOUT TO GRADUATE FROM THE University of Tulsa and face the challenge of job hunting. I had frequently called CKLW radio in Detroit for reports on the auto industry union negotiations. I figured the station was way out of my league. Its fifty-thousand-watt AM signal penetrated the Detroit market, the state of Michigan, and every state between there and Florida. It also could be heard across four Canadian provinces.

When I flew there, I was in awe. The format—both the 20/20 news and the uptempo rock-and-roll sound, were like KAKC's, and so tightly produced and error free that I knew I was tackling a big assignment in coming there.

The 20/20 news format was a creation of Los Angeles radio programmer Bill Drake, who figured there was such a tune-out factor on rock-and-roll stations when the news was done at the top and bottom of the hour, that sliding it in at twenty minutes past or twenty minutes before the hour would still comply with the broadcasting regulations, and keep the audience tuned in for the music. Drake was correct beyond anyone's imagination, as stations like KAKC, CKLW, WHBQ in Memphis, WRKO in Boston, KHJ in Los Angeles, and KFRC in San Francisco saw their numbers dramatically increase.

I remember meeting with CKLW News Director Don West and assistant news director Byron MacGregor in June of 1969 at a Windsor, Ontario, tavern. MacGregor, a twenty-one-year-old Canadian, was a big guy with a booming voice. He had befriended many of the new employees at "CK" in his two years there, and I was no exception.

They hired me on the spot at the tavern, and Byron had offered to let me share his apartment in Windsor. Little did I know what a great friendship we were going to have. Byron liked the ladies, and he liked his Molson beers. That combination, plus the fact that we shared the upper room of a small penthouse at Windsor's Holiday Inn overlooking the Motor City, created some interesting moments.

After an evening of partying, Byron was not the easiest guy to roust for work. He worked early mornings and I worked until late at night. Around 4:30 A.M. the alarm would go off, Byron would be sawing logs in a deep sleep, and I'd wake up (of course), turn his alarm off, get up, and go over to his bed to try to roust him. Then at 4:45 A.M. the station would call, I'd answer, and still there was no discernible movement out of Byron.

Finally, about 5:10 A.M. the Holiday Inn security guard, like clockwork, would pay us a visit, lift the already clothed-from-the-night-before Byron up, and help him down the stairs to the living room. Byron would reach out for a beer from the refrigerator in his still-asleep state and finally become ambulatory as he jumped in the CKLW Camaro and headed down the four blocks to work.

At the station, he'd grab the copy from the overnight editor, charge into the recording booth just as the three gongs of the CKLW news jingle went off, plop down in the chair, and boom out, "It's twenty minutes before six, this is Byron MacGregor, CKLW 20/20 news . . ."

And MacGregor did it day after day.

One time Byron went to a big meeting in Windsor put on by the Ford Motor Company, with a who's who of Ford executives from both Detroit and Windsor in attendance. Everybody came dressed in suits. Byron was on his best behavior. But that was about to change.

Byron MacGregor (right) and Bob outside CKLW in Windsor.

Lunch seemed to be going perfectly. Byron was in true form—telling stories to all who would listen to him at his table for ten. Little did he know he was being stalked.

A pint-sized guy from the mailroom at the local paper, perhaps not as endeared to Byron's sizable radio audience as others, picked up a cherry tomato from his salad. He studied it for a minute, then looked over at Byron about twenty feet away.

He couldn't resist. His arm drew back, his body pivoted slightly in the chair, and suddenly the cherry tomato was released like a missile. Byron never saw it coming as it smashed into his nose and fell to his plate. War had been declared!

Byron leapt to his feet, and the rather stuffy luncheon was about to get some real entertainment.

The big Canadian went under, over, and around the tables, weaving like a football running back on his way to the end zone, in hot pursuit of his quarry, who had fled the room.

He was gaining ground as he bolted through the front doors of the building and down the sidewalk, his long strides narrowing the gap on this annoying little urchin who had dared to ruin his day.

He was closing the distance between them to just a few feet as he rounded a corner of the building at full speed, his gaze fixed on his prey.

He never saw the punch that hit him.

Another guy from the paper, about the size of a five-story building, served up a fist sandwich to Byron as he rounded the corner.

It had all been a set-up to bait Byron into running into the trap.

A mortal man of less stature than Byron would have been knocked out, or at least would have laid still for a moment to check for missing teeth and to try to figure out where the train came from that hit him.

Not Byron, though. Like a coiled rattlesnake, he sprang back up, lunging at what looked like Andre the Giant.

Behind Byron, with a death grip on his shirt tail, was CKLW news director Don West. He was skidding back and forth on the

A former roommate and wonderful friend Byron MacGregor, his wife Jo-Jo (well-known Detroit broadcaster in her own right), another longtime friend from CKLW, (now WWJ-Detroit newscaster), Joe Donovan, and Bob, 1994.

pavement in his slick-soled dress shoes, looking like a snow skier out of control, in a futile attempt to hang on to Byron and prevent a free-for-all.

Then the police arrived.

It looked like a scene from *West Side Story* where the street punks plow through the trash cans in an alley, leap some chain-link fences, and vanish into the night. Only this time, everyone had on a suit and tie. Nevertheless, they had escaped and the Byron MacGregor World Championship Street Fighting Match had suddenly been declared a draw.

In 1970 Byron was named news director at CKLW, and deservedly so.

For my part, I had proved I could survive the Canadian winters and thrive in a major radio market, but I missed Tulsa and my friends, and I moved back to KAKC for what turned out to be a three-month stint in early 1971.

It was a remarkable relationship that Byron and I shared. He married a lovely woman, Detroit broadcaster Jo-Jo Shutty, in 1976, and the three of us got together for visits several times over the next twenty years.

No one who really got to know him could ever forget the many kind deeds he did, including the gift to the Red Cross of every cent he made from the successful 1973 narrative record, "The Americans." The Canadian-born MacGregor took a stand against anti-American sentiment, and with the record's success, left a memorable legacy by praising Americans for helping Canadians and the world in times of trouble.

Byron left us far too soon.

He died from pneumonia in Detroit in January of 1995 at age forty-six. His funeral service included a who's who of CKLW stars from over the years. He was a great human being, and we shared some of the best times of my life.

C H A P T E R   S E V E N

Meet Mr. Polyester

IN MID-1971, AFTER A SHORT STINT AT KAKC, I JOINED another Tulsa radio station, fifty-thousand-watt KRMG. There I got my first real chance to be a radio reporter.

I did everything—traffic reports from cars, planes, and even helicopters. I covered the school board, the police beat, and chased fire engines until people must have thought I worked for the fire department.

The traffic reports could be a challenge. There were days in the winter when I would be driving down an ice-coated street, steering with my elbow while turning the toggle switches on and off as the police and fire scanners blared, and all the while holding the microphone for my traffic guest. I was using the other hand to turn the car radio up and down to make sure I didn't get any feedback from the radio.

I was the most dangerous thing out on the road. In fact, one time I even had to report my own wreck! (Remember, I'm the kid that flunked the driver's test three times.) I was doing my juggling act with all the switches on the police scanners while trying to drive with my knees. Amazingly, I was still in the proper lane of traffic. Suddenly, I heard a "thud" and realized I'd been sideswiped. The other driver pulled over to the curb behind me as I somewhat sheepishly told the radio audience, "Folks, I think you

Yours truly, "Bob-In-Traffic" as I was known in my traffic reporting stints on KRMG Radio in Tulsa, applying the boot—literally—to the station mobile unit after I got it stuck in the mud for the umpteenth time.

may want to avoid the far right lane northbound at thirteenth and Lewis Avenue. I'm currently blocking the traffic in that lane."

Another time I was covering some flooding conditions late one night and drove my own Oldsmobile Cutlass into six feet of water.

"Honestly," as I told the wrecker driver who was trying to locate my car beneath the water, "I thought the road went straight ahead."

Unfortunately, the road, and I guess you could say the car, took a dip . . . a big dip, and I had to climb out the window as the car was sinking. The water eventually receded, revealing my new giant bathtub. Amazingly, after the muck and mud was cleared from the cylinders, the car ran for another seven years.

In fact, it was the same car I used to pick up my leap-year date in February 1976. Early that year KRMG decided to hold a contest to get me a date. (I must have looked desperate.) The program director, Jerry Vaughn, announced that women could write in, enclose a picture, and tell why they wanted a date with Bob Losure.

The winner would be picked up in a limousine, be presented with roses, and be escorted by me to a college basketball game followed by a late-night dinner at Tulsa's exclusive and private Petroleum Club.

I figured I had the advantage because my prospective dates could send in their pictures, but they wouldn't know what I looked like. Then Jerry and I would go through the letters and pictures and I'd pick my date.

Then I came up with what seemed to be a brilliant idea. Why not tell the radio audience that Jerry was going to make the final decision? That way, the pressure was off of me, and I could call four or five of the other girls I wanted to go out with and say, "Gee, I'm sorry, it was Jerry's pick. You were really the one I wanted." What a plan!

A girl by the name of Kim Basinger (no, not the winner of the '97 Academy Award for Best Supporting Actress, but a star in her own right) sent a cute picture and concluded her entry letter with, "I want to make this a night that you'll remember, Bob."

Contest over. We had a winner.

I had a great time on that date, and Kim and I went out several times. I also dated two of the other entrants. Eventually I couldn't stand the guilt and told them the whole story. They all let me in on a little secret: I hadn't fooled them for a minute.

KRMG radio not only helped me get a few dates here and there, it led me down the road toward television.

In 1975 I was asked to do a weekly public affairs show for the Tulsa County Bar Association on what was then KTEW, the local NBC television affiliate.

Keep in mind, my formal wardrobe consisted of polyester leisure suits and two-tone shoes. My hair was parted in the middle and I was wearing a gold-fill chain around my neck. But since I was doing the show for free, the gentleman producing the show, Gene Dennison, overlooked all that.

The other Kim Basinger.

The show was taped during the week and played on Saturday afternoon as part of the station's community programming to satisfy the Federal Communications Commission requirements. I first started off with some fairly simple, and somewhat non-controversial themes—looking at the role of the district attorney, the police chief, and the public defender's office. Unfortunately, in my enthusiasm to "break new ground" I soon trampled on the rather conservative nature of this public affairs show.

I brought on a guy to talk about marijuana reform, then he and I followed it up with a two-part exploration, or perhaps exploitation of prostitution in Tulsa.

My guest cohost on the three shows was attorney Rabon Martin, who to this day calls them as he sees them. So here we were in the conservative Midwest in 1975, trying to ask questions like we thought Phil Donahue would do it, with a prostitute silhouetted against a black background.

I'll give Rabon credit for one thing—his knowledge of the prostitution business was formidable. He knew just what questions to ask to get us taken off the air in a hurry.

The icing on the cake was a multipart question from Rabon's fertile mind on what the client could and could not request of the prostitute, and the going price on the street for each of those services.

We were soon out on the street ourselves. I am fairly certain that the station management made its decision before the station I.D. played at the close of the final show.

I was not about to give up on television, though. I had spent ten years in radio news, and it was time to move on. Television news seemed the obvious path for me.

"Prince Valiant" with my checked suit and striped tie outside KRMG Radio mobile unit, 1975.

In August of 1976 I heard about a job opening for a reporter's position at KOTV, the CBS television affiliate in Tulsa, and I wasn't going to take no for an answer.

KOTV had just hired Jack Bowen, an anchor from Oklahoma City, to be their news director. Since the previous news director, Clayton Vaughn, hadn't expressed any interest in me, I thought this might be a chance to break into televison broadcasting.

I found out that the station's general manager, Duane Harm, knew of my work in radio news, so I called him. He said he'd be glad to introduce me. Jack, on the other hand, didn't know me, but to appease the general manager, he sent photographer John Bateman and me over to the fire department to do a story. That was no problem.

Then he asked me to go into the studio and pretend to read a newscast. That was a problem.

The word amateur comes to mind to describe how I read from the prompter that day. My anchor style was so monotonous that when I exited the anchor set and crawled back to the director's booth, even Jack Bowen had become my victim.

Mouth agape, head firmly back in the chair at least momentarily, Jack had succumbed to an overwhelming desire to sleep.

My voice really had lulled him to sleep. So I did the only prudent thing. I shut up.

The silence woke him up immediately.

I half-heartedly asked him when I should call back. His answer was less than thrilling.

"How about if I call you, Bob?"

He never called. In fact, he may have been so depressed over knowing that I was on the streets impersonating a journalist that he quit.

"He's not here. He went back to Oklahoma City," the receptionist replied when I called KOTV two weeks later. I told her she must be kidding, that Jack had been working there only three weeks. She told me she wasn't kidding.

I was shocked. I wanted to find out what happened, so she put Duane Harm on the line.

" Mr. Harm, is Mr. Bowen no longer there?" I asked.

"Well, sometimes those things don't work out, Bob."

"Who is your new news director then?"

"Bob, I've decided to go with Doug Dodd. He's been a reporter here for some time. He's done a good job."

"How interesting!" I replied. "Doug Dodd you say? He and I went to school together at TU. We're fraternity brothers from Pi Kappa Alpha. I'd be pleased to work with Doug."

Neither one of us talked for maybe ten seconds. Then Duane made his fatal mistake. He spoke first.

"Bob, I don't want to be presumptuous here . . . but . . . uh . . . was Jack leaning toward hiring you?"

All I could think of was Jack in that chair, leaning way back.

"I may be a little presumptuous here, Mr. Harm, but I thought he was definitely leaning . . . over . . . uh . . . that way."

"Well, how much was Jack going to pay you?" Duane asked.

Now was no time to be greedy.

"Gee, I really don't know. I think we were talking about . . . maybe . . . fourteen thousand."

Duane suddenly had a new reporter. I started October 18, 1976.

CHAPTER EIGHT

There's No Business Like the News Business

EVEN IF I HAD A FACE MEANT FOR RADIO, I WAS SURE I could succeed in TV. For one thing, I was familiar with writing a radio story, putting a couple of comments from the interviewees in the report, and leaving it at that. If I didn't have the pictures to go with the sound, so what? Even if the natural sound of the emergency vehicles and people screaming at a fire scene was excellent, nothing was more important than my own narrative.

Eventually, I began to catch on to the fact that television is more than radio with pictures.

Even though my salary of fourteen thousand a year was not exactly going to put me on the *Forbes* 400 list, I assumed the folks who were watching me on TV didn't know that. They might have thought I was making six-figures, at least until they saw me on camera.

With my wrinkle-free polyester leisure suit, two-tone shoes, and nearly shoulder-length hair parted in the middle, absolutely no one could possibly think I was capable of being paid at all.

I did hang on, though, and within two years I was anchoring the weekend newscasts. That also involved editing some of the videotape, writing and producing both the 5:00 P.M. and 10:00 P.M. newscasts, perhaps even interviewing newsmakers for the show, and then trying to act bright and perky and warm and cuddly for the audience.

I had to be all things to all people. I would be told to be enthusiastic yet conservative, authoritative yet warm. All I could think of was to develop three or four more personalities that would fade in and out as a I read the news, thus allowing me to literally be all things to all people.

A year and a half into my weekend anchoring stint, I got a lucky break. Three dominoes fell all at once. Longtime anchor Clayton Vaughn left to anchor at the Public Broadcasting System TV station in New Jersey, WNET, which was a great move to the New York City area.

Former Cleveland, Ohio, anchor Jim Hale, who had also worked in Boston, St. Louis, and Dallas, was brought in. He lasted nine months. He missed the big city and went back to Cleveland and worked in radio there for many years.

The next occupant of the anchor chair was former KOTV anchor Bill Pitcock, who got a ton of publicity because he was returning to the anchor chair he occupied alongside Clayton for many years.

He showed up on a Monday and quit on a Friday . . . of the same week.

He discovered what a lot of anchors realized in the 1970s—if they left television for a few years, and then returned, it just wasn't the same. Some of the fun of having parties with your coworkers and not worrying about being replaced was gone. News directors were constantly doing that frenetic impression of "Murphy Brown's" former news director, Miles Silverberg, keeping you guessing on whether the latest ratings slide would propel you out the back door. There were also big consulting firms hired by these television conglomerates, ready to take the opinions of focus groups of twenty to thirty people to decide what personnel changes needed to be made.

They would be told to look at tapes of several anchors, then judge which ones they liked best. It meant that a thumbs down signal from the focus group, despite an anchor's longevity on camera in a city, could put that anchor out on the street. The consulting firms also realized that unless there was a constant recommendation to move anchors in and out of different cities, then the consulting firm might lose its job.

Bob trying to get a frog scared enough to jump farther than a frog has ever thought of jumping before, at a Tulsa radio station promotion in 1979.

In many cases, news directors were, and still are today, given mandates to do whatever it takes to be number one. With that sometimes comes an expanded budget, and the new news director suddenly has the bucks to lure an anchor from a competing station in the market—adding not only a recognizable talent, but automatically drawing a talent that was helping a competing station.

Of course, management could also put enough money on the table to lure a homegrown talent back home from a bigger city, and that's just what KOTV did with Clayton Vaughn in 1979, just a little over a year and a half after he left.

I had been the so-called "interim anchorman" on the early and late news at KOTV for several months. I detested the feeling that I was good enough to fill-in, but only until the station got a "real" anchor. Then in October of '79, with just a twenty-four-hour notice from the station's general manager, I went from anchoring the high-profile weeknights newscasts to the lower-profile weekend anchoring and weekday reporting.

It wasn't a pretty scene, either. The station had invited five hundred media and advertising executives from the Tulsa community to hear the announcement in a local hotel ballroom. There I was on stage, glad-handed by the general manager who told the audience what a good interim anchor I had been. Then Clayton was introduced as the returning hero. I suddenly looked like the eighth runner-up in a beauty contest. In fact, I think the stage grew smaller as I seemed to get closer and closer to the back door.

Clayton told the audience that it was indeed great to be back home, and I'm sure he meant it. That was 1979. He stayed in that anchor chair until 1997.

I had learned a valuable lesson in broadcasting. Keep your eyes and ears open to what top executives are saying behind your back, and if you hear a rumor about yourself, it's probably true. To add a couple of thoughts to that—never assume you'll be promoted unless you have it in writing, and save some money for the lean times.

Fortunately, about a year later Clayton's co-anchor, Melanie Roberts, moved on, and I filled her slot for the next five years. I finally felt like I was part of the station's future.

KOTV was the first television station to go on the air in Tulsa in 1949. On the thirtieth anniversary, I was assigned to do a historical perspective on the people who had worked there, and it was quite an impressive list of people.

Harry Volkman, the first weatherman at KOTV in 1952, has been a weatherman in Chicago television for decades. Jim Ruddle, another KOTV anchor in the late 1950s, also made his mark in Chicago at the anchor desk.

Jim Hartz, who cohosted the "Today Show" with Barbara Walters for several years in the 1970s, had anchored at KOTV in the early 60s. In fact, his big break came not from any mass mailing of his audition tapes, but on a fluke.

A recruiter from NBC was coming through Tulsa on his way somewhere else when he got snowed in. So he turned on the local news in his hotel room, liked the friendliness and warmth that the native Tulsan projected, and hired the twenty-something Hartz to anchor at WNBC in New York.

One guy who stands out among reporters is ABC "20/20" reporter Bob Brown, who was a few years ahead of me at Edison, and quite far ahead when it came to making a story come alive in the viewer's mind.

He grew up working at KAKC Radio. I worked there four years after he left. Then he went to the University of Tulsa. I followed. He went to KOTV as a reporter, and I got there a few years after he departed. So I'm still on his trail, but ABC's "20/20" program hasn't called yet.

In the retrospective I produced, I discovered a guy named Robert Reitz who did the weather in 1956. The face on the picture looked real familiar, so I contacted former KOTV promotions and programming staff member Joyce Bachus, who first came there in 1954.

She looked at the picture, and remembered that he was the guy who wanted to be on Broadway.

I was busting at the seams wanting to know.

He left KOTV to start his Broadway acting career in 1957. He changed his name while he was changing jobs, too. He was Robert Reed . . . the father on "The Brady Bunch."

Next I discovered a round-faced fellow who did a kids show. His face looked familiar too. It was Spanky McFarland, years after playing "Spanky" on Hal Roach's "Our Gang of Little Rascals."

Two Tulsans who began their TV careers behind the camera at KOTV were actors Gary Busey and Gailard Sartain. Busey continues to get top billing in numerous movies and made-for-TV projects. Sartain was a cast member for years on the hugely successful "Hee Haw" syndicated program, and landed a significant role a few years ago as the rather bucolic husband of Academy Award winner Kathy Bates in the movie *Fried Green Tomatoes*. Both were studio cameramen on KOTV, and their original claim to fame was as actors on a Saturday late-night KOTV show that they, along with their friend, Jim Millaway, put together each week.

They had to dream up the skits, write down where they wanted to go with the show in sometimes an improvisational style, then do "The Uncanny Film Festival and Camp Meeting" show live. It was on KOTV, and later KTUL in Tulsa 1969–1973.

It reminded me at the time of some of the "Honeymooners" shows that Jackie Gleason and Art Carney would do live. Gailard once told me that if the clock in the studio said they had three minutes to fill, and the skit was about to come to a close with no script left, they'd simply "fake it" the rest of the way, making up the lines as they went.

One man who was on hand to see just about all that history being made was my friend, Henry Lile.

There is no one whom I've ever met who was kinder and more caring about what happened to me and anyone else he came in contact with than Henry. He worked at Tulsa's Rainbow Bread Company for many years, and added two more jobs—as pilot and photographer for KOTV in 1954.

He and I probably spent literally a thousand days and nights riding around in a KOTV van, listening to the police scanner while gobbling down ice cream in between the hundreds of stories we covered together.

Henry was well into his fifties when he and I started working together in 1976. He was at KOTV, still trudging through the rain, sleet, and snow into his late sixties, and died just shy of his eightieth birthday.

His sense of humor lives on to this day in the many stories of his exploits. My longtime friend and former KOTV reporter Susan Bunn recounted to me that just after sunrise one day, Henry was flying her to the scene of a story when he asked her if she'd like to see the sunset.

She responded, "How do you propose to do that, Henry?"

Suddenly, the plane rolled upside down, Henry's hands firmly on the stick, as the startled reporter saw the sun seeming to set on the horizon.

Then there was KOTV sportscaster Ken Broo. Big. Tough. Rugged . . . But unfortunately for him, apprehensive about flying, and putty in the hands of one Henry Lile. As Henry was taxiing down the runway one crisp fall Saturday morning to get Ken to the OU–Nebraska game at Norman, Oklahoma, he got a thought.

Anchor Melanie Roberts, weatherman Lee Woodard, Bob, and Ken Broo during my interim anchoring days at KOTV in 1979.

"Ken," he drawled. "I've been feeling poorly the last couple of days and I want you to know something before we take off today. You know, if I were to die in a flaming crash today, there'd be a little item at the bottom of the obituary column, saying 'KOTV Pilot Killed In Small Plane Crash. Services Pending.' But Ken, if *YOU* were to die in the crash with me, there would be a big banner headline all over the front of the paper—'Famous Sportscaster Dies In Flaming Air Disaster!'"

Broo flung open the door of the taxiing plane and ran over two hundred yards back to the terminal, and perhaps beyond. The OU–Nebraska game was about to go on without Ken Broo's coverage.

Henry couldn't believe what had happened. Two weeks later, after numerous apologies from Henry, Ken forgave him.

Another story that will always stand out in my mind concerned a trick that Henry and KOTV weatherman Lee Woodward pulled on anchorman Bill Pitcock. Henry had flown to Okeene, Oklahoma, one day to shoot some footage of the annual Okeene Rattlesnake Round Up. This is an annual event in which grown men poke around under rocks with long sticks, hoping to annoy some Diamondback Rattlesnake long enough that he'll come out, attempt to kill them, and in the process be killed and made into a small meal, or perhaps a belt.

Henry bought one of the captured four-foot snakes, had its mouth taped up, and brought it back, still wriggling, to surprise Bill for his birthday. Then Henry and Woody (Lee Woodward) got the absolutely brilliant idea to put it in a box, wrap it up with a little bow on top, and give it to Bill on the air and see what happened when he opened the box.

The trap was set. Bill, or " The Moose" as he was affectionately known, was a strapping six-foot-three-inch guy with a big, booming voice. And here he was, absolutely delighted and so happy that Woody and Henry had bought him a birthday present and were giving it to him on the air.

"For me?" he exclaimed, as he ripped at the wrapping.

Henry and Woody were about to bust a gut.

Bill lovingly caressed the top of the box. He gently lifted the top, inch-by-inch, his smile to the camera getting broader by the second. He slowly moved his head, peering around the lid at the wonderful surprise that awaited him.

The coiled snake exploded out of the box, its taped mouth bouncing off Bill's arm.

Bill bolted from the set, screaming.

He went through one door, then two doors, then finally out the back door, racing for his car with Woody and Henry in pursuit. The director, with no one left on the anchor set, faded to a commercial break. Two minutes later, he faded to another break. Still no Bill Pitcock.

Meanwhile, out in the parking lot, hands in a praying position, Woody and Henry were only partially stifling their laughter, pleading with Bill not to get into his car and drive off. They were sorry. They would never think of doing anything that nasty again. They'd even box up the snake and take it all the way back to Okeene right now if necessary. Oh, they wanted Bill to "say it ain't so" and just come back inside.

Bill finally got his heart rate somewhere close to normal and stormed past Henry and Woody to go back inside—five commercial breaks in a row later. It was the first and last on air appearance at KOTV by a venomous reptile.

CHAPTER NINE

Live at 5:00
—Dead by 5:30

LIVE TELEVISION NEWS MIGHT BE DESCRIBED AS A HAND grenade waiting to go off. You may have to wait for two weeks for a real gem of a faux pas (that's French for screw-up) to appear on a local or national newscast, but when it does, it gets dubbed on seemingly every blooper reel in America.

I was filling in as the weatherman on KOTV many years ago, and a fax from the Associated Press of a woman who was blown sideways by sixty-mile-an-hour winds in Boston fascinated me. She was perpendicular to the street, her skirt hiked up just above the knees, and it must have taken some great photography to catch her in midair. Fortunately she wasn't hurt.

I had the fax mounted to some cardboard, and a camera in the studio was to shoot it, have it chroma-keyed up on the weather map behind me during the newscast, and point out how windy it was in Boston that day.

At the juncture I should explain that most weathercasters can't turn around and see the local, state, or regional maps behind them. An electronic device called a chroma-key removes all the light blue color from the wall behind you (so you can't wear a light blue suit), then electronically puts the image on the wall in place of the blue color so the home viewer can see the map. For the weathercaster to see the image, they have to look at TV monitors either recessed into the wall or mounted sideways next to the map on each end, and turned inward so the weathercaster can see where he or she is in relation to the map.

My vision just wasn't that good that night.

I called for the picture of the Boston woman to be superimposed behind me, but I wasn't sure whether the director of the show had done it. So, I kept inching closer to the monitor to the side of the wall, unable to distinguish the picture until . . .

It looked like I was trying to peek up the woman's skirt!

The anchor crew was giggling audibly. Then to add to my predicament, I jumped back when I saw where I was.

Laughter again erupted.

"Can we have the next weather map please?" I demanded, partially stifling a giggle myself.

I swore off doing the weather ever again.

Little did I know we were going to have another side-splitting time on that same weather set just four years later, on Halloween night, 1983.

I was anchoring the 5:00 P.M. news, and introduced meteorologist Jim Giles, a highly respected prognosticator who has been at KOTV many years. As I introduced him, I turned to my right . . . and nearly fell out of the anchor chair.

Jim had a giant black cape draped around him. He also had an equally bizarre-looking Mr. Potato Head nose and glasses that would have made the Marx Brothers proud.

I did a double take as I looked at him, then asked him where he got his costume, and could he get his money back if he took it back to the store right now? He laughed, and I followed up with a question about whether it might rain on the trick or treaters.

"No, Bob, it's smooth sailing tonight for those little ghosts and goblins," he replied. As Jim turned to the national weather map, a cameraman suddenly held up a sign next to the camera . . . and he wasn't kidding:

SEVERE WEATHER STATEMENT FROM THE NATIONAL WEATHER SERVICE IN 30 SECONDS.

Jim sputtered. His eyes widened to the size of saucers behind Mr. Potato Head. He struck me as looking like a clown that had been hired for a children's party, but accidentally entered the door of the funeral parlor next door during a service.

"Well, boys and girls. What do you know? The National Weather Service has pulled a surprise on us. We have a bulletin on a severe thunderstorm warning coming up in just a few seconds," he blurted out.

The bulletin was read by the National Weather Service spokesman as Jim turned to me, a look of helplessness etched on his face. I felt sorry for him. How could he have known?

"Do you think it's too late to take off the cape?" he inquired. His plea was like rearranging the deck chairs as the *Titanic* was going down. We were, at that moment, sinking with our own little *Titanic*.

Jim never dressed in costume on Halloween again.

I also had the pleasure of working with Wilbert Moore, a photographer for KOTV, and though he was no saint, he could be funny and charming, and he was certainly never dull. In fact, he was a rarity in broadcasting.

He had served time in the federal pen at Leavenworth, Kansas.

What he was in for I never knew or cared to know. Looking back, perhaps that was the best way to leave it. Wilbert could be somewhat moody.

One night he was videotaping a small segment of a Ray Charles concert in Tulsa for the late news. After asking someone in Ray Charles's entourage for the best location to shoot from, he got permission to set up his camera in the middle of the auditorium. Then the story got interesting. Two minutes before Ray was to sit down at the piano on stage, Ray's road manager came out to tell Wilbert to move his camera to the side of the auditorium.

Now, you could ask Wilbert, or you could humor Wilbert, but you could not demand something *of* Wilbert.

Wilbert became more than a little agitated. Suddenly he pulled a switchblade knife out of his pocket and began twirling it around in his hand, instructing Charles's manager to either let him stay, or step outside. The manager looked at the knife in stark terror, looked back at Wilbert, and disappeared into the wings of the theater in the blink of an eye, along with about four rows of patrons.

So, as Ray Charles was playing "Hit the Road Jack," Wilbert was still in the middle of the auditorium, camera firmly planted for an outstanding shot of the stage, the only remaining patron in the middle of the auditorium.

No police ever showed up. Perhaps it was because there was no one left to call them. I'm not sure Ray Charles knows to this day what happened. My guess is that Wilbert probably even got his autograph before the night was over.

Of course, videotaping a concert for editing later is one thing, but covering a concert live can be full of even bigger obstacles.

Back in the 1950s and 60s, KOTV had prided itself on having a full-size mobile studio, complete with studio-size cameras that could cover everything live from the opening of an airport to a football game. As time went on, and national programming from the networks replaced local programs, the big live trucks became dinosaurs. It was not until 1978 that KOTV re-entered the business of having a scaled-down live truck, which was to be used for news exclusively.

Our first assignment was not really news, but the opening night of Ziegfield's (not to be confused with New York's legendary Ziegfeld's), a glitzy club for live performances on Tulsa's southeast side. So, like that rare occasion when the sun, the moon, and the earth all aligning themselves for a cosmic show, so it was that the fabulous entertainer Tina Turner, newsman Bob Losure, and a live report in twenty-degree weather with snow falling would come together with near disastrous results.

Tina was to perform two evening shows, one at 8:15, the other at 10:15, and I was to do a live report with videotape from her 8:15 show, and a live interview with her between shows on the 10:00 news.

Then two problems developed . . . at 9:45, just fifteen minutes before we were to go on live, we found out that the floor-waxing crew earlier in the day had put down too much varnish on the stage, so much that it resembled a thick, gooey mixture of Coke syrup mixed with Super-Glue. So as Tina Turner was doing her dance numbers, she occasionally resembled a chicken high-stepping around the barnyard as she tried to keep her high heels from becoming monuments stuck to the stage. Then the second problem became apparent. We didn't have enough cable to extend from the live truck to our camera that would be backstage.

At 9:55 Ziegfield's PR Director Mark Cortner came up with what he thought was a brilliant idea, and since we had just five minutes until the live report, any idea looked brilliant. Mark pointed out that we could use the cable we had to reach directly into Tina's dressing room, which was at the side of the building.

We scrambled around to the side of the building, my photographer's light on top of his camera guiding us through the darkness. There was no time to waste.

It was now 9:59 and we were leading off the newscast.

Then it dawned on me. It was twenty degrees. It was snowing. We were actually going to have the gall to bust in like Eliot Ness and the Untouchables into the dressing room of *the* Tina Turner, who had already experienced a Super-Glue-kind-of-night on stage. To top it off, we were going to bring the twenty-degree weather, the snow, and a glaring light right through that door with us like some TV crew exposing a filthy restaurant kitchen.

It was 10:00 straight up. Clayton Vaughn began the newscast.

"We now go to Bob Losure who's standing by *live* at Ziegfield's, a new entertainment club celebrating its inaugural night, where Tina Turner is doing two shows. Bob, I can see you, but where are you? It looks like you're out in a back alley somewhere."

"Clayton, we're just about to enter Tina Turner's dressing room!"

I was sinking fast. Cortner was behind me trying to get the master key into the lock.

I turned around. Cortner, looking like a burglar in a tux, clicked back the bolt with his master key. He swung back the door and it banged against the wall.

Every single pearly white in Tina Turner's mouth was visible. I expected a scream to come out at any second.

"Hello, Miss Turner, I'm Bob Losure with channel six. Sorry to barge into your dressing room like this, but we . . . uh . . . just wanted. . . ."

Tina Turner, dressed only in a terry cloth robe, turned quickly from the full-length mirror before her, placed her comb on the dresser, and stopped me in midsentence.

"Well, boys! Please have a seat on the couch. Is this a live interview?"

"Yes Ma'am. We just wanted to know how you like being in Tulsa, and . . ."

Again she took control.

"Great little city you have here! You know, I'm on the road forty-five weeks a year, and the hospitality. . . ."

I wouldn't have blamed Tina if she had shot me.

She was the consummate professional. She was oblivious of the cold air and the bright light in her eyes. She wasn't about to let us, or her audience, down.

Unfortunately, that wasn't the last time we'd face a panic in the chill of a cold spell on KOTV.

It was the first weekend in April 1984—Springtime. Clayton, meteorologist Jim Giles, sportscaster Bill Teegins, and I were headed to the Azalea Festival Parade in Muskogee, Oklahoma. Muskogee is a small, but historic place forty miles southeast of Tulsa, known for its Honor Heights Park, a beautiful spot that's bursting with colorful azaleas each spring.

We were to make one lap through the park at the head of the parade, waving at our admiring fans, with the warm sun beating down on the convertible loaned to us by a local car dealer. What could go wrong?

I'll tell you what. The azaleas were freezing their little buds off. The wind chill was close to zero, and here we were, four frozen

"The Four Frozen Amigos." Bob, KOTV co-anchor Clayton Vaughn, sportscaster Bill Teegins, and meteorologist Jim Giles just before the ill-fated 1983 Azalea Festival Parade.

stiffs, in parkas, in an open convertible, leading a parade of frozen horses, frozen bands, and frozen cheerleaders.

Then it got worse. The whole extravaganza was supposed to be televised by KOTV, but someone left the microwave transmitting unit on a tin roof that had already been heated up to sizzling temperatures by the sun.

No more microwave unit.

So off we went around the park at the front of the parade anyway, as the station substituted the parade coverage on the air with "Fat Albert and the Cosby Kids."

We were just about finished motoring through the park, when suddenly the producer signaled to us from the main reviewing stand: "Go around again! We've got a new microwave unit and we're back in business."

Now we needed a bulletproof canopy on the car. As we rolled along at five miles an hour, waving at the same people we had passed just forty-five minutes before, people started leaving the reviewing stands. Some were pointing at us and shaking their heads in bewilderment. A couple of them booed. They were—perhaps correctly—assuming that our giant egos had not been fed with just one lap around the park. No, we were going to make an Olympic marathon out of this.

To make matters worse, we had caught up with The Royal Lippizon Stallions, or whatever the mounted horse brigade was.

As we dragged the parade around the park with us, it was apparent that the horses had fought the good fight, but they needed relief . . . *now.* Suddenly we were bumping over piles of poop.

Then the car died. I mean that convertible wouldn't start, and that led to the *final insult.* As the fragrant aroma from the horses wafted up around us, the KOTV cameras began zooming in.

We were trying to smile, but our faces were frozen into a Mount Rushmore pose.

"What are we going to do?" Teegins asked dejectedly from the backseat.

It was a great question. No one had an answer.

So we calmly opened the car doors, stepped gingerly around the horse poop, crossed the finish line, and kept waving as we melted into the crowd . . . on frostbitten feet.

CHAPTER TEN

My Battle
with the *Big C*

I HOPE THIS CHAPTER WILL NOT FRIGHTEN YOU OR MAKE
you uneasy with the topic of testicular cancer. It was April 1985,
and one night I was, shall we say, rearranging things below the
belt. I felt something odd, like three large marbles laid end-to-end
in the scrotum sac. One of my testicles was three times the size of
the other. I ignored it.

I chalked it up to age (I was thirty-seven), but two weeks later
it had doubled again in size. There was no pain, but all the same I
was worried. I went to see my doctor and he sent me directly to
urologist Dr. David Confer on another floor of the same Springer
Clinic in Tulsa.

Two days later Dr. Confer did a simple operation to remove
the right testicle. Forty-eight hours later the results showed it
was an embryonal cell carcinoma, meaning it was cancerous, and
had possibly spread into my lymph nodes in my stomach and
chest.

I was concerned, but not yet worried. I was told I had a good
chance of recovery if the extent of the cancer could be determined
right now.

I wondered how I had contracted the disease—was it a genet-
ic trait? Perhaps stress in my life was causing the cells to divide
irregularly?

Whatever the cause, I was getting the message loud and clear that people who say that they never think about death are only delaying the inevitable, or perhaps are naive enough to assume they don't have to worry about it before they're seventy-five. I tell you truthfully that the news from Dr. Confer had my stomach in knots, and it had me thinking of who should be put in charge of caring for my mother if I wasn't around. I also began to think about what people might say at my funeral.

It was probably good that I didn't have a whole lot of time to think about everything before the next surgery. Dr. Confer did a masterful job of keeping me from getting too apprenhensive about the next, more complicated procedure. He would sit at the window of his office, thumbing through the pages of a medical book, shake his head in agreement, then turn to me and soothingly say, "I think we can have you out of the hospital within a week." I knew nothing about the operation that lay ahead and that was probably just as well too.

Within days I was under the knife again, this time with a sixteen-inch incision beginning under my right arm, across my chest, and down below my belly button in what is called a "lymph node dissection." Two of the seventy lymph nodes removed were cancerous, indicating the cancer was on the move toward my lungs and brain.

The lymph node dissection was a major operation, and I laid in intensive care at Saint Francis Hospital in Tulsa for two days with numerous tubes coming out of my body. One of them was a nasal-gastrointestinal tube that ran from a loud machine all the way up my nose, and down into my stomach, withdrawing the material that couldn't pass through my intestines because they weren't ready to function yet. By the beginning of the third day, I was moved into a private room, still with the tube in my nose. The tube made me very uncomfortable, irritating my nose and causing a somewhat gagging sensation in my throat. I was told that if I pulled the tube out, I might choke to death, and just the fear of this made me sleep in fitfull twenty-minute spurts in intensive care that first night. The second night I was in a regular room, but I still couldn't sleep. All the Morphine and Demerol I was receiving made the TV set in the corner of my hospital room start multiplying into six TVs. And soon, those TVs seemed to be circling around the room. It was like being in a bad dream and not being able to wake up. I came to realize that some people do better on pain medication than others and I was on of those who just gets scared when their mind starts wandering out of control. I asked for a portable fan. For the first and only time in the hospital, the nurse deserted me. I yelled for help, then asked to see the nursing supervisor. She arrived quickly and I told her of my problem with the other nurse, and pleaded for a fan. It was there and running in five minutes.

Finally on the fifth day in the hospital I fell into a deep sleep and awoke about 9:00 the next morning. For some reason, I had a feeling that there was something *different*. I felt my nose. There was no tube in it. I looked down. Eighteen inches of gastrointestinal tubing lay in my lap.

During the night, I had yanked the tubing out through my nose. I was still breathing . . . fortunately.

A nurse came in, shocked at what I had done. She told me she would help me put the tube back up my nose, down my throat, and into my stomach. I declined the offer. In fact I think I said something like "over my dead body."

I had her call Dr. Confer. He said to wait a few minutes before doing anything with the tube.

Soon, I detected faint signs that my intestines were grumbling. I looked at the ceiling and whispered a quiet, "Thank You, Lord."

Within days I was out of the hospital, but I was not out of the woods yet. Dr. Confer, who's assessment of the situation turned out to be right, recommended that I start chemotherapy immediately. My oncologist, and today my longtime friend, Dr. Alan Keller, told me I could either go back to work and have a 60 percent chance the cancer wouldn't come back, or endure the chemotherapy treatments now, and be fairly certain the cancer would not return.

I went back to work, figuring that I'd lose my job if I stayed away for the expected three months of chemotherapy treatments. Of course, with all the information I had heard about the nausea with chemotherapy treatments, I was in no hurry to begin them.

A local disc jockey, Johnny Rivers, cohosted the Jerry Lewis Labor Day Muscular Dystrophy Telethon on KOTV with me each

Tulsa radio personality Johnny Rivers, Jerry Lewis, and Bob at a break during
preparatory meetings for the annual Labor Day Muscular Dystrophy Telethon in
Las Vegas, 1985.

year, and he and I headed to Las Vegas in late July '85 for the
annual gathering of telethon hosts with Jerry Lewis. Lewis was
and is a great cheerleader and motivator and his down-to-earth
presentation made all of us proud to be a part of the fundraising
for a cure for all neuromuscular diseases ranging from ALS to
Muscular Dystrophy. I stood there hoping I wouldn't have to have
my own private telethon if the cancer returned in my body.

The decision was soon made for me. A month later, the cancer
returned as a lump the size of a quarter in my pelvic region. I went
under the knife immediately to have it removed. Now, I had no
choice. I'd have to take as many chemotherapy treatments as my
body could stand. After the third operation, I emceed the MDA
Telethon on KOTV and entered the hospital two days later for the
first chemotherapy treatment.

Through the Testicular Cancer Resource Center in San Antonio,
Texas, and my link to the Internet (losure@boblosure.com), I
frequently hear from men of all ages who, like me, don't want to
admit that the elongating testicle inside the scrotum sac could be
testicular cancer. Just the fear of surgery and the greater fear of

what they've heard about chemotherapy treatments makes them hesitate to see a doctor. I say to them, "Don't wait another day." Think for a minute about those that love you. The fear can be conquered if you just get rid of any guilt for waiting so long, and see a urologist or oncologist.

For those who currently have cancer, I want you to take comfort in the fact that chemotherapy science has advanced significantly since my battle in 1985. Antinausea drugs like Zofran, and improved chemo drugs, which didn't exist then, today make over 80 percent of chemotherapy treatment an outpatient procedure, done while you're sitting in a comfortable lounger. It's seldom more than four hours for two days a week.

When I went in to Saint Francis Hospital in Tulsa with my testicular cancer, the procedure involved large bags of fluids and chemotherapy drugs and three antinausea drugs injected intravenously for twenty-four hours a day for five straight days.

Everyone reacts differently to different drugs. Some people sailed through the process even then. My sailing went through some stormy weather. One of the antinausea drugs, Reglan, sent me up the wall. In fact, there were times I thought I could climb the wall, walk across the ceiling, come down the wall like Spiderman, and then do it all again. I became nervous, agitated, and began crying for no reason at all. Some people have no reaction to Reglan.

I didn't feel sorry for myself, and I wasn't concerned with the giant incision across my chest, but for some reason, I didn't care to see anyone in the hospital except for my mother and the nurses. The nursing staff understood how I felt, and it was not easy for them either, since they had to insert a needle the size of a jackhammer in my arm two or three times during each five-day period to start the chemotherapy into my body. I think their compassion, understanding, and cheerfulness, despite the sadness of seeing some patients die before their eyes, deserves all the thanks we can give them. They had the kind of attitude that made me want to fight the cancer, and I think my body, despite all this toxic fluid killing some good cells with the bad cells, responded to those positive thoughts coming from my brain and from my wonderful caregivers.

The 1985 Muscular Dystrophy Telethon on KOTV in Tulsa just before I re-entered the hospital for chemotherapy treatments.

While I couldn't figure out what was making me so nervous in the first chemo session, by the second chemo session three weeks later, it was beginning to be obvious that the Reglan was hitting me like a bullet. In the second session the nurses responded with Nimbutol suppositories—two of them—to put me out. I slept for forty-eight hours, with large bags of chemotherapy drugs feeding into me. Twice I climbed the rails of the bed and plummeted to the floor in my grogginess, as I searched on hands and knees for the bathroom. Fortunately, the nurses responded in time. They reduced the level of knockout drugs. By the third session, the suppository dosage was cut by more than half and the process worked. Still, it was five days of going in and out of sleep every few hours and enduring the uncomfortable needles.

Meanwhile, I had been watching television . . . a lot . . . and I didn't like what I saw after I finished just my first chemo session. My replacements—two attractive women—were on the air, and doing an admirable job. And from what I heard behind the scenes, they had signed contracts and wouldn't be moving out of the weeknight anchoring positions anytime soon.

I had an agent in New York, Conrad Shadlen, who had already been looking nationwide for a year. I began calling stations on my own from my hospital bed. One day Conrad called and said CNN Headline News had an opening. Could I get to Atlanta between the first and second chemo sessions to audition?

I said, "How about yesterday?"

I arrived at the old TBS-CNN building at 1050 Techwood Drive in Atlanta. A tall, slender man was walking toward me from the parking lot. As he approached, I realized who he was. I opened my mouth to speak, but nothing came out. He passed right by me, nodding and moving toward the building. It was Ted Turner. Later I discovered that the Braves were on a losing streak, and Ted had been in the clubhouse just moments before having a heart-to-heart talk with the team. Good thing I was dumbstruck.

My audition was full of insecurities. First of all, my hair was falling out—due to the first session of chemo, so I did my best to keep some of it on my head. I also looked like a refugee from some third-world country. I was gaunt, my shirt was real loose around my neck, and I was worried about having enough breath. I told the news director of Headline News, Paul Amos, the truth—I was going through chemo, and I could be there in three months—assuming I lived. I charged into the audition copy during a break on the Headline News set.

As I paused at the end of a sentence, Paul stuck his head out of the control booth and peered at me around the corner.

"Faster," he said. I picked up the pace to 180 words a minute. He apparently liked it. Or maybe he felt empathy for my condition, or both. After a slowdown in the talks between Paul and Conrad three weeks after the audition, I called up Paul myself.

Paul was empathetic with my desire to show him what I could do for CNN. He called Conrad within a week, and I was hired.

Years later, I found out that Paul had lost his mother to cancer.

Meanwhile, back in Tulsa, my longtime friend and photographer from KOTV, Henry Lile, was doing his best to cheer me up.

Henry always mowed the landing strip and nearby grounds at Harvey Young Airport on Tulsa's east side. One day while I was

A photo of KOTV photographer Henry Lile's grass artwork.

undergoing chemotherapy, he mowed around a giant pattern that he had laid out across two acres of the airport. In huge, one hundred-foot-tall letters, he had mowed a message of hope:

"GET WELL BOB."

It was visible to planes for miles away.

He even flew his plane over the field, camera in hand, and took a photo of his work, then blew it up to an eight-by-ten size. He brought it to me at the hospital, and it really made my day.

By now, I was ready for a fourth session of chemo. I remember walking into the hospital, a pillow under one arm, an egg-crate mattress under the other, and plopping down in Dr. Keller's office in the hospital. Was my white blood cell count (the one that drops precipitously when you take chemo drugs) high enough? For a moment, Dr. Keller studied the chart results for signs of any cancer. He put his hand to his chin, and wheeled around to face me.

"Bob, I think you've had enough. You're going to be all right."

I was, as they say, *on top of the world*. If I could conquer cancer, I could conquer anything I set out to do.

Dr. Keller's news that I could resume a normal life still left some unanswered questions. As happy as I was to be going to Atlanta and CNN, could I get over leaving my lifelong friends and my mother after over thirty years there?

There was also the question in October 1985 whether KOTV management would let me out of my contract, which ran until June 1986. In retrospect, I could have saved any worrying I did on that subject.

When I walked through the front door of KOTV on my way to see the general manager, I suddenly realized I was like the ghost of Jacob Marley, from Dickens's *A Christmas Carol*. There I was on their doorstep, and I was doing management the biggest public relations favor they could ever imagine. I was asking to break a contract, and they were more than willing to oblige.

Soon I was boarding a plane for Atlanta.

KOTV's hiring of replacements during my cancer treatment actually made the transition to a new job much easier. I had needed some fresh air and a new challenge for some time, and CNN was that new challenge.

I had honestly believed all along, even lying there on the floor of the hospital, that my time on earth was not up yet, and that when it was, I'd be given the time to resolve it inside. I had faith in Dr. Keller's honesty. He has had the unfortunate task over the years of telling hundreds of people who were dying to get their affairs in order.

Anchoring from the old Headline News set at 1050 Techwood Drive in Atlanta. Yes, I wore a hairpiece for a few months in 1986 until my hair grew back.

One of them was the guy I had worked with briefly at the start of my KOTV journey, Bill Pitcock, who encouraged me every step of the way in my fight with cancer. Four years later he fought valiantly with stomach cancer and died within two months of diagnosis.

Another co-anchor I had the pleasure to work with, Ramona Huffman, had a wonderful sweetness about her that radiated to everyone she met. She battled colon cancer for three years. She fought on bravely, bedridden and weighing less than one-hundred pounds in the final months at her mother's home in her hometown of Malvern, Arkansas, before succumbing. The source of the cancer could never be found.

Hal O'Haloran, a veteran sportscaster in Tulsa, had multiple problems of liver cancer, diabetes, and heart disease. Even as he battled all of those, he was the first person to come to Saint Francis Hospital to drop off Dan Rather's *The Camera Never Blinks* and to tell me what was going on in Tulsa broadcasting. He passed on within a few months of my recovery.

Yet for every story of a friend I've lost to cancer, there is a story of a success. In December 1997 I was at a Christmas party in Tulsa and a man came up to me and looked at me with an expression of astonishment combined with happiness on his face.

"Are you Bob Losure?" he inquired. "I've got a story I've been waiting to tell you."

His name was Bill Hamilton, and in 1995 he and his son, Steve, were driving from Tulsa up to Bartlesville, a town about sixty miles north of Tulsa, to attend an air show. He told me that as he and his son were driving along, they heard KRMG morning personality John Ehrling interviewing me about my fight with testicular cancer.

Steve, then twenty-seven, turned to his father and confided in him somewhat reluctantly, "Dad, I think I've had a knot in my groin area for about two weeks. I wonder if it could be . . ." and his voice trailed off.

Bill Hamilton wasted no time. Steve was examined at Saint Francis Hospital almost immediately, and indeed his suspicions were correct—he had testicular cancer like I had experienced. The only difference was that he and his father were smart enough to get it examined weeks earlier than I had done, so Steve never had to have a lymph node dissection, never had the cancer return, and never had to go through chemotherapy. Today Steve travels across the globe as a freelance photographer.

Steve represents a lot of Americans, both men and women, who have great lives ahead of them if they'll do the annual physicals and pay attention to any changes in their bodies. Do you want to know why the Testicular Cancer Resource Center in San Antonio, Texas, seems to be working so well and why other similar services with e-mail addresses are helping to save lives everyday? I think it's because we have a stigma that there's something we've done wrong to deserve the cancer, and it's best not to embarass ourselves or put the problem in the lap of our loved ones. Let me tell you—death will come to us soon enough, so why unnecessarily deprive those who care about us? We are on this earth to enjoy life, and should not let guilt over a disease ruin our pursuit of happiness.

CHAPTER ELEVEN

Two Weddings and a Funeral

"SON, YOU'RE IN TOO MUCH OF A HURRY. TRY SLOWING your life down by about 25 percent, and you'll make a lot fewer mistakes."

That was my dad, Homer Losure, when I was twelve. I hate to admit it, but the man was on target. I had always wanted to do everything before the sun went down.

For instance, I once was married for six weeks.

The next time I was married for six years.

Believe it or not, there was a lot to be said for the six-week marriage versus the six-year one. The first time, we cut our losses and split up. The second time, I had all of this guilt about failing the first time, so I hung around, making my wife miserable, my friends wishing they could be in the witness protection program, and twelve angry men and women in the divorce trial wish they had never moved to my county.

My second wife was a knockout in high school, and I think she still is. She was a skilled baton twirler, and I was simply too shy to ask her out. She had two girls who were nine and fourteen.

We were both thirty-eight when I ran into her at the twentieth reunion of the Edison High School Class of 1965. I was recovering from my second cancer operation and she was teaching nursing at the college level. By November of 1985 I had the job at CNN in

The couple "in happier times," as they always say. Next to me is my second wife, Kathy, her oldest daughter, Paige, and Paige's now-husband, Jeff. We rafted down the Nantahala River in North Carolina that day in 1990.

hand, and I was convinced I didn't want to move to Atlanta without her. We were married in May of '86.

In hindsight, we didn't know each other that well. She had given me a great deal of support through those days and nights when my life, my manhood, and my job future were in question.

She was taking a big gamble and making a huge sacrifice in leaving a good job and uprooting her girls for a move—seven hundred miles away. Looking back, there would never have been a way to find out if the relationship would really work if she didn't move to Atlanta.

We found out it didn't work, and that's the end of that story.

Now, you may be wondering why I did a take-off on the Hugh Grant movie and titled this chapter "Two Weddings and a Funeral." Actually, I originally wanted to call it "Three Ministers and a Wedding" because of my first marriage, but then the funeral story came up, I shared it with the relatives closest to the deceased, and they decided it would be OK to put in the book.

Mistakes are nothing new to me, and fortunately I usually learn from them, however hard the lesson is. For example, how many of you have ever attended the wrong funeral?

Well, I confess that I have.

It was Christmastime, 1997. A good friend of mine, a photographer from the television days at KOTV, was back in Tulsa to visit his mother, who had been in declining health for some time. He and I got together for lunch the Tuesday before Christmas, and it wasn't four hours later that he called me to say she had suffered a terrible stroke that afternoon and died.

The funeral was set for the Saturday after Christmas at Memorial Park Chapel in Tulsa. I got directions to the chapel, and on my way down the road I saw a fellow directing traffic into what looked like the chapel. I pulled in, drove to the front of the parking lot, and about three cars parked behind me. It was 10:40 A.M. The funeral was not to start until 11:00.

So I walked in the chapel, moved to the end of a pew, and looked around for anyone I might know among the mourners.

I looked to the left, then peered over my shoulder to the four rows behind me, then back to the front. No, there was no one I knew.

Suddenly the minister began the service.

"We are here today to remember the great person that *Ed* was," he intoned.

Ed who? I thought to myself.

Whose funeral is this anyway? I don't know any Ed!

Then I did the only sensible thing to do. I got up in the middle of the sermon and trampled across everybody in that aisle.

"Excuse me sir . . . uh, pardon me ma'am . . . very, very sorry about this . . . whoops, is that your foot?"

The minister began talking louder.

I reached the end of the row, head bowed . . . and stumbled into the aisle, catching myself on the arm of the pew. I scurried up the aisle like a moviegoer on a mission for a box of popcorn so as not to miss any of the movie.

As I reached the lobby, I turned right and entered an office, my gaze meeting the eyes of a surprised young woman.

"Miss, I'm afraid I'm at the wrong funeral," I blurted out, my face growing redder by the minute.

She stared back in disbelief.

"Exactly what funeral were you going to, sir?"

"Uuuh . . . it's the one at the Memorial Gardens Chapel . . . I think."

"Sir, just take a left out on the road when you go out the front door, and follow the path. I'd say it's about four hundred yards down there."

It was now 10:55 A.M. I rushed to the car. Then I stopped. The car was blocked in by all those other cars that had parked behind me!

Think. Quick. Just five minutes to double-time it four hundred yards in a suit, in freezing weather.

I arrived, huffing and puffing. I grabbed the giant ring on the chapel's large wooden door. I swung it open . . . but I lost my grip.

Bang!

The door hit the chapel's stone exterior like a sledgehammer, and a giant mass of cold air rushed in on top of the assembled mourners.

In the short span of maybe fifteen minutes, perhaps unheard of in modern times, I had managed to disrupt two funerals.

It could only happen to me.

At least I had made it to the right funeral.

Now the story of my *first* marriage—the six-week one. If you blinked, you might have missed it.

It was April 1983. Former KOTV anchor Bill Pitcock called me one day and said he had a beautiful twenty-four-year-old University of Texas graduate that he wanted me to meet.

Bill knew Nina's father from their partnership in the oil business, and said she had an interest in perhaps getting into broadcasting.

So we met at a downtown Tulsa restaurant. I was immediately intrigued by this smart, attractive young woman. There was something about her that promised more to life than I had ever seen before. I was smitten as the term goes. One month later I proposed marriage to Nina. Unfortunately for her, she accepted, and in that moment we were both surely guilty of some kind of crime.

I asked her father for her hand just days later. I think it took years off his life—but he made the sacrifice. The wedding date was

My first wife, Nina, with me at the Fairmont Hotel, San Francisco, 1983.

set for October first. Between those two dates, a strange set of warning signs occurred—not unlike the lookouts must have felt as the *Titanic* entered the iceberg field, but I ignored them all.

Suddenly, my little wood-frame house and yard were undergoing huge changes. She was on a mission to change her man and his abode. Gone were the refrigerator and one of my window air-conditioning units.

Then the shrubs around the house were yanked out and replaced with a desert southwest look of large gravel with a few small plants yearning for water. In fact, I got thirsty everytime I looked at the landscaping . . . thirsty for getting my money back.

She was on fire with ideas. Soon, my house was repainted inside and out. Then my wardrobe got a makeover (admittedly, both my house and wardrobe desperately needed a makeover). Finally, the makeover extended to my friends. If she didn't like them, I needed to lose them. And I almost did.

With just two weeks before the wedding, as plans for three ministers, ten groomsmen, ten bridesmaids, ten ushers, and six hundred guests were in their final stages—a dose of reality set in. No, a little backbone hadn't suddenly broken through yet, but I realized my dad was right. In my haste to do everything before the sun went down, I was throwing caution to the wind.

To add to the higher and higher stakes of all this, my betrothed told a stadium-sized crowd of eighty-eight at the wedding rehearsal dinner that I had promised her a very special wedding gift—a dark brown Mercedes!

I once heard a female friend of mine tell me of her own wedding—"I knew when I was walking down the aisle that it wasn't going to work."

How could anyone do something so stupid, I thought.

Suddenly, as I stood there before God and half the inhabitants of the earth that day in October 1983, I realized the word stupid had taken up permanent residence in my brain.

After all that landscaping, painting, new appliances, and new furniture, I couldn't have come up with the money for a tricycle. I had borrowed and borrowed for months. I think I had a credit card from every bank in America. And therein, lay the seeds for disaster.

At the ceremony in Tulsa, I think we had everything but ten lords 'a leaping. It was an absolutely grandiose affair that sparkled in every way. Only the two principals knew the truth.

My longtime friend, Tulsa attorney Lonny Davis, was also at the ceremony. Sort of. After helping to usher everyone in at the wedding, he sneaked out to the church's lobby, found a nice cozy little office, and set up his portable TV to watch a world championship soccer game. Perhaps he already knew the outcome of the wedding, and it was only the soccer game that was in doubt.

Very quickly, the honeymoon was over. She was jealous, perhaps because many of the women at the wedding were ones I had dated. So when we arrived at San Francisco's Saint Francis Hotel for the honeymoon, you'll probably guess what happened. I had barely reached the reservation counter when a woman I didn't recognize threw her arms around me.

"Bob, it's so good to see you!" she exclaimed. "I haven't seen you out in the longest time in Tulsa! We'll have to get together while I'm here . . ." I then showed the young lady my wedding ring. Unfortunately, Nina had not stayed around for that part. She had adjourned to the wedding suite, her jealousy raging.

Six weeks later, as our debts mounted, she and I realized that there was no pot of gold for either one of us. She left and went back home to her parents, thinking perhaps that I would beg her to come back. I, instead, called my lawyer.

Then I went to many of my friends to beg their forgiveness for the way I had alienated many of them.

She got married a few years later. I honestly hope it's been a happy marriage for her. Her determination to succeed in everything she does, plus her striking good looks, should serve her well.

Ironically, I was TV channel surfing one day a few years ago, when up popped a familiar face on the game show "Family Feud." I rubbed my eyes. No, she was still there. It was Nina, showing off her beautiful smile—with her new husband, her brother, and her mother—all jumping up and down in what can only be described as "Family Feud" ecstasy! They'd won the big jackpot! She had finally found a way to get that dark brown Mercedes!

CHAPTER TWELVE

Anchors Say the Darndest Things

ANCHORING LIVE TELEVISION NEWS REALLY GIVES THE "bloopers" people a field day, especially since news and sports shows generally are the only ones that are live anymore. There was a veteran noon anchorman on a local Atlanta station a few years ago who had just finished his weather forecast and was headed back into the news segment, when he was handed one of those "just in" notes. He correctly ad-libbed that a former football hero from the University of Georgia in the 1940s, a Heisman Trophy winner, had passed on. He then deadpanned that the deceased was "seventy degrees." Then without skipping a beat, he went on to other news.

During the commercial break, the anchor was told what he had said. The commercial break ended, the anchor was back on camera, and he apologized, adding, "What we meant to say was, 'He was seventy degrees.'"

By now, the deceased probably was at room temperature or below. The anchor had done it again. Station management reportedly presented him with an unexpected, but perhaps badly needed two weeks off immediately following the newscast.

Journalists slip up in the area of history too, even when it's recent history.

An anchor was reading a story a few years ago on an Oklahoma City station about native Oklahoma actor Ridge Bond, the rugged cowboy character "Curly" in the first performance of the musical *Oklahoma* on Broadway. He was to be honored for the 1944 stage role by the Oklahoma Heritage Hall of Fame in Oklahoma City.

Then the writer's knowledge of history got a little fuzzy.

"Bond will be inducted into the Hall of Fame tonight," the announcer proclaimed. "He played the part of 'Curly,' one of the Three Stooges, longer than anyone else."

You don't have to be reading the news live to find yourself in a predicament either. My statuesque Headline News anchor colleague Lynne Russell, who I get asked about more than any other CNN or Headline News anchor, always tries to stay ahead of a potential disaster on the news set.

She refuses to read the copy off the electronic teleprompter unless she has the paper copy in her hand—just in case the teleprompter suddenly fails. She's not bluffing either. If the story doesn't make it into her hands before the tally light on top of the camera comes on to tell her she's on the air, she'll simply disregard the teleprompter and read whatever looks good from other stories she has in her hand. Producers may pull their hair out because they couldn't get the so-called *hard copy* to her in time, but Lynne is consistent and goes pretty well unchallenged. She simply

The CNN Headline News anchor team in 1988. On the back row: Bob, Lynne Russell, Dave Michaels, Don Harrison, and David Goodnow. On the front row: Cindy Klose, Chuck Roberts, Bobbie Battista, and Lyn Vaughn.

doesn't want to go blindly reading news copy that could, and has, stopped in the middle of a sentence because of one technical foulup or another.

She's the subject of numerous articles, and appeared in *Atlanta Magazine*'s April 1995, issue a couple of years ago. On the cover she was shown in what looked to be a patent leather outfit with fishnet hose and one leg hiked up and touching her other knee. Inside the magazine, photos of her with her husband in a formal dining atmosphere; in a karate gee; and on her side, dress raised high to reveal the now-famous thigh holster.

For those of you who missed the show, she showed up on "Late Night with Conan O'Brien" on NBC a couple of years ago. O'Brien questioned her about her work as a part-time private eye and sheriff's deputy, and her skill at being a ballerina on one hand, and a tough-as-nails black belt in *tai chi* on the other.

"Yes, we catch philandering husbands all the time in my private detective work," she said. "Of course, we do most of it with long-range lenses on the cameras, so it's seldom I have to get involved with actually serving them the lawsuit."

Then Conan asked the inevitable question about how she's able to hide her nine-millimeter thigh holster and pistol when she's in a dress.

That, of course, elicited a few whistles as Lynne used her charm to bring the audience into the tent: "Can I really do this on television?" she said somewhat bashfully. "This could get me fired, you know. Actually, it's quite simple to hide it. . . ."

At that point she slowly began to raise her dress, and for those men watching the Conan O'Brien that night, time suddenly stood still. For one brief moment in time, the show had the full attention of every male who was watching across America.

Lynne continued hiking up her dress, revealing the holster and gun. She unsnapped the holster, then snapped it back again.

No wonder she gets so much respect from the floor crew when she sits down in the anchor chair.

For almost fifty years, Art Linkletter has made a living off his original "Kids Say the Darndest Things," then reviving it every few years—because kids in an unrehearsed situation still give us our most honest look at the world around us.

So it is with anchors and reporters. Sometimes we fail in our unrehearsed, unedited live situations on location, and sometimes we succeed.

In October of 1989 I was sitting at home in Atlanta watching the pregame show before the start of the World Series, and suddenly saw ABC's Al Michael's describing the undulating shaking of the stands, the power outages across a wide area, and the fires blazing in San Francisco's Marina District. Little did I know I'd be standing next to those burned out buildings the following night, getting reports that ninety people had died, then having to reverse myself the next hour and say the death toll had just been lowered to sixty.

It was a very eerie feeling in the darkness of a normally bustling city like San Francisco, with only a few lights from emergency generators on. Add to that the fact that I was standing right next to thirty-five other reporters, all lined up like some chorus line, each of us talking simultaneously at the beginning of each hour and half-hour. Twenty feet from me stood Peter Jennings and Tom Brokaw. Concentration was the key. If I had been distracted for a second by the reporter barking out his or her script, I would never have recovered, given this rock concert level of reporter mania.

In fact, our communication lines in those early days of CNN Newsource, were so primitive that at one point, we had to synchronize our watches in San Francisco with WWOR TV in New York.

WWOR TV wanted to do a customized live report with us in San Francisco. When I say "customized," I mean that anchor Roland Smith would announce at approximately 11:01:00 P.M. on the East Coast that "Bob Losure is now here to give us an update on the casualty figures from San Francisco. . . ."

I would thank Roland, introduce my report complete with soundbites and video that our crew had put together, then close out the report standing in front of the fires in the Marina District. Roland would say "thank you" and go on to his next story.

There was one giant problem however. I wouldn't be able to hear Roland because my IFB, or Interrupted Feedback Device, couldn't be wired to the WWOR signal. So we synchronized our watches with New York, and in the dark, in the midst of chaos, we tried our luck.

With no one to listen to, just dead silence, I took the field producer's drop-of-the-hand cue at exactly 11:01 P.M. and began with, "Thank you, Roland. Here in San Francisco. . . ."

I don't know how it worked, but it did.

His intro ended at the precise second that I began by thanking him. Fortunately, we never had to do that again, and the audience never knew that I didn't see or hear Roland Smith at all that night.

In 1989, a devastating tornado plowed through a busy commercial area of Huntsville, Alabama, flattening buildings and killing nine people. It alternately rained, then sleeted, then snowed while I was doing my daytime live reports from the main commercial area that had been devastated. As night fell, our generators had to be used for the lights, and we had to make do with what we could find for electricity for the reports themselves. That happened to be an electrical box from a steakhouse that had been blown over. We hooked up our lights and cameras. Then we routed the device to the IFB, so that I could hear myself and other anchors introducing me from other cities.

It was cold, it was windy, and it was pitch black when the anchors in West Palm Beach, Florida, said, "We now go live to Bob Losure in Huntsville for this update on the deadly tornado there."

I responded with, "That's right, Tom and Mary, nine people are dead. . . ."

No sooner did I get those words out than a gravelly toned voice blared into my ear.

"Hey, Mac," he yelled as my IFB reverberated.

" I need an order to go. Give me three chicken fried steaks, four baked potatoes . . . Oh yeah, how about two of those cobettes. . . ."

By now I was thinking: Did I say sixteen people were injured or sixteen cobettes were injured?

The one-way conversation continued.

"Hey, can you hear me? It sounds like some guy is broadcasting the news. . . ."

All I could think about was to keep right on talking, even if the words didn't make any sense. It was like the lyrics, "Row, row, row your boat . . ." while a chorus of ten people are joining in every five seconds. I had to remember that only I could hear him, and nobody else.

He finally gave up, because I heard a dial tone for the rest of my report.

It is at those moments when you are tested to see if you have the "right stuff" to anchor when everything else around you is going south. My colleague at Headline News, Don Harrison, survived an even bigger test less than a year later.

It was 1990, and President Bush, through jet lag or sleep deprivation, had collapsed at a dinner in Tokyo, falling beneath the table, and there were several minutes when the world didn't know how serious his dilemma was.

And therein, lies the basis for this story.

That morning, shortly after the President collapsed, a phone call was made to a CNN medical reporter at CNN world headquarters in Atlanta. The caller, purporting to be the President's physician, Dr. Burton Lee, told the reporter that he wanted to let CNN know first that the President had died.

The reporter, thinking that he had a major story, turned to his computer, opened up the "Read-Me" file where CNN employees are alerted on company business and news judgment calls. He typed in the statement that he had word from a man, purporting to be the President's doctor, that President Bush had died.

The rather gray area of all this is that at the time, in 1990, there were no hard-and-fast rules of what was and was not supposed to go on air from the "Read-Me" file.

Immediately, two CNN vice-presidents descended on the CNN medical reporter's office to find out what was going on. At Headline News, two floors below, where the normal supervising producer—Dave Willis—was in a meeting, the less-experienced line producer in the director's booth noticed what was going on. Through the IFB communication line to anchor Don Harrison on the set, the line producer asked Don to read the bulletin in the "Read-Me" file as soon as the report then playing ended.

Don, with thirty-five years in TV news behind him, argued that there was no corroboration of the statement from any other news sources, so he didn't feel Headline News should air it.

Now, that's where this story should have ended, because in most local newsrooms, the main anchor's experience gives him or her a certain degree of latitude to decide such issues. However, at Headline News, and at CNN for that matter, there has always been a rush for each to beat the other with a major bulletin, even if it's by a scant fifteen seconds.

So the line producer raced out of the director's booth, down the hall, and into the office of the senior producer. Third in the management hierarchy at Headline News, the senior producer got just a quick briefing, and in his haste to get the story on the air ahead of CNN, told Don to read it.

So, here was Don Harrison—a man in a quandary. If he didn't read it and it was true, he'd be accused of insubordination. If he did read it, and the story proved to be a hoax, he'd know what it felt like to be the captain of the *Titanic* shortly after hitting that iceberg.

The tally light on the top of the studio camera came on, and there sat Don Harrison . . . stuck in the twilight zone.

He stalled for a few seconds, saying, "There has been a report of tragic news involving the President . . . and we have no corroboration on it yet . . . no confirmation from The White House. Nothing from the Associated Press . . . no word from Reuters. . . ."

Just as he was about to include the fact that his third cousin had not confirmed the story either, the senior producer began waving frantically at Harrison from out of camera range, but within Don's peripheral vision, pleading with him to forget the story.

It had just been stricken from the "Read-Me" file by the CNN team upstairs.

Harrison glanced incredulously at the senior producer and returned his gaze to the camera.

"We'll have that news a little later on for you," he said. "Let's go to the business desk in New York now, to get the latest on trading at the opening of today's session. . . ."

The President, as we all know, was not dead. The call was later traced to a phone used by a mental patient in Idaho. It was not the President's doctor.

Don Harrison had saved the network. Both current and former CNN and Headline News employees might still be wearing brown paper sacks over their heads with little holes punched out for the eyes if Harrison had not vamped for a few seconds.

TIME, Newsweek, and other magazine reporters were watching though, and were quick to point out the near calamity. CNN's public relations spin on it was that an alert producer had stepped in to save Don. Actually, Don, by stalling for just a minute, saved us all.

As Paul Harvey, also a native Tulsan, might put it: "And now you know the rest of the story. . . ."

CHAPTER THIRTEEN

Who Could Ever Forget Ted Turner?

IN THE EARLY DAYS OF CNN, IN THE BASEMENT OF A former country club at 1050 Techwood Drive near downtown Atlanta, there was a feeling of camaraderie that was unique. CNN and Headline News were much smaller than they are today and were separated only by a hallway.

Ted Turner even lived in the building part of the time in a penthouse suite. In the middle of the night, I'd be anchoring on the overnight shift and suddenly Ted would stroll by in his pajamas on his way to the twenty-four-hour snack shop. He'd stop in, stand by the set, and bark out, "Hey, how do you get the energy to read all that stuff over and over like that?"

"It's my job Ted and you're paying me for it," I'd reply.

"Oh, that's right," he'd drawl. "Have a good night, Bob."

Sadly, in some ways, those days of being the underdog "Chicken Noodle Network" are history, and Ted skulking around in his robe at four in the morning will only be a story to be told among aging CNN staffers.

By the middle of 1986, Ted was building new CNN facilities inside a portion of a large gray stone monolith called the Omni. He had bought the building with its fourteen-story atrium, hotel, and business offices in 1985. Like so many times before, he went out on a limb financially to reconstruct a corner of the Omni where "The World of Sid and Marty Krofft" had been, into his state-of-the-art headquarters for CNN. He brought in security personnel and a police precinct. Where there was empty space from high-end retailers who had failed, he filled it with fast food restaurants for the rising number of conventioneers coming to the World Congress Center next door.

So instead of bumper cars and video games in the eight-story indoor amusement park that Sid and Marty Krofft had constructed, a four-story glass and steel enclosed set of studios now dominated the atrium of the Omni, drawing hundreds of thousands of visitors to the news mecca for tours each year.

In early 1987, just months before CNN was scheduled to make the move to the Omni, I had a couple of friends in town and we were—what else—touring the future CNN headquarters. As I pointed up to the construction site three levels above me in the atrium of the Omni, a little voice over my shoulder whispered, "Do you think they'll ever finish this thing?"

It didn't look like they were going to finish it to be perfectly honest, but without even turning around I told the stranger, "If Ted does something, he makes the deadline." Then I turned around.

It was Ted.

We both smiled. The only difference between us—I was the one with the red face. He strolled away with Liz Wickersham, an anchor from our New York entertainment bureau, on his arm.

A year later I was sitting alone at a Chinese restaurant in the Omni. I finished my meal and rose to walk to the cashier's desk, when a loud southern drawl suddenly pierced the cacophony of the lunch crowd.

"Hey, Bob! You're doin' a good job, buddy. Keep it up!"

E. F. Hutton had just spoken, and a room of about ninety people got as quiet as if they were in a library. The "Chairman of the Board" was at it again.

I waved at Ted somewhat sheepishly from across the room, then approached his table, extended my hand, and thanked him for the compliment. Then I wheeled around, shoulders squared, head high, feet not even touching the floor, and made my triumphant exit. He had made my day.

It doesn't take a brain surgeon to see that Ted is liked in many quarters because he calls it the way he sees it. He's also lived a charmed life, which has been described as a startling series of narrowly missed disasters. When he skippered his yacht in Britain's prestigious Fastnet race in 1979, he was so absorbed in victory that he didn't even know a gale was killing fifteen yachtsmen in the boats behind him.

Risks, whether in the water or on land, were not new to him. In 1970 he bought WJRJ, channel 17 in Atlanta, renamed it WTCG (later WTBS), then bought dirt-cheap reruns of former network shows like "Leave It to Beaver" and transmitted them from his earth stations to satellites in a time when cable was just in its infancy. He single-handedly changed the face of television, in part thanks to another Tulsan who helped him with his satellite transmissions, Ed Taylor.

Ted first became a national figure in 1977 when he won the America's Cup yacht race with his ship *Courageous,* then showed up at the victorious press conference, champagne bottle in hand, under the table. Part of the problem, according to Atlanta psychiatrist Dr. Frank Pittman, was Ted's worry that he would die at age fifty-three. His father had committed suicide at that age, and it deeply affected Ted in terms of worrying about his own mortality.

By 1985, Dr. Pittman had convinced Ted to take lithium to control his wide mood swings. Suddenly he was no longer afraid of dying tragically. But his risk taking never abated.

In 1985 he unsuccessfully tried to buy CBS, and his attempt not only generated a panic stock repurchase move by CBS, it gained him the publicity he wanted.

In 1986 his costly acquisition of the Metro-Goldwyn Meyer (MGM) movie library for $1.2 billion was considered foolish at the time. Yet, the purchase brought him two great allies who came to his aid—Telecommunications Incorporated and Time-Warner. It also meant that they could control the free-wheeling nature of Turner's spending. Within two years they were lending support to his debut of Turner Network Television (TNT) to get the movies from the MGM library on the air on their cable systems.

It would be hard to find anyone else in American history who has made almost everything he's touched turn to gold. Turner's team, the Atlanta Braves, are perennial World Series contenders. His investment in a few buffalo in Florida in 1976 has grown into the nation's largest buffalo herd, with fifteen thousand head of bison on ranches in Montana, Nebraska, and New Mexico. Perhaps in just a few years, with the herd growing by 25 percent a year, a "Ted Turner Bison Burger" may be a staple in America.

He's a healthier man today than he was ten years ago. He's stopped drinking. He and his wife Jane Fonda even find time to hike, ride bicycles, hunt, and fish.

Just like his decision one weekend in 1996 to become a part of Time-Warner, his decision to give one hundred million dollars to the United Nations for the next ten years probably doesn't surprise those closest to him. They're used to surprises.

I saw Ted probably nine or ten times in the more than eleven years I worked at CNN. He always addressed me by name, and wanted to know how I was doing. I truly appreciated that. I know he cares about what happens at CNN, because its startup in 1980 was also against all odds. It is, in many ways, still the truest reflection of his success.

I only hope that Ted, as vice-chairman of Time-Warner, will see that CNN's ethics remain high, and that the staff gets the financial and promotional support it needs to be the world's news leader.

CHAPTER FOURTEEN

Breaking Up
Is Hard to Do

WHEN I BEGAN ANCHORING AND WORKING BEHIND THE scenes at Headline News in January 1986, I was thankful to have a job, much less one with a network that was on the rise. Being replaced as a main anchor at the CBS television affiliate in Tulsa had actually caused me to finally make a move that I had been reluctant to make for a long time.

However, there was one problem that never went away. I thought I was hired to be a full-time anchor *weekdays*, but it never happened. No one lied to me directly—not Headline News Vice-President Paul Amos nor my agent Conrad Shadlen, but my contract called for primarily anchor duties. Yet there was a little caveat in the contract that said I might be performing "any journalistic duty." That could range from writing to producing, watching news conferences and pulling clips of what the newsmakers said, and basically just about anything short of wallpapering and tile cleaning.

There was a function called package producing in which I would, for example, look at a WGN TV tape sent by satellite from Chicago. It would show flooding in Sioux City, Iowa, complete with soundbites and voice-over footage, and could be supplemented with perhaps copy from the Associated Press wire or another news service. Simple enough. But it proved to be part of what I saw as a fork in the road that led me down a path lined with confrontations. My assumption that I would be anchoring full-time on Headline News provided a valuable lesson: *Don't assume anything. Get it in writing or it may never happen.*

From the beginning of my tenure there, January 6, 1986, until May 7, 1997, I anchored Saturdays and Sundays, then filled in for ill or vacationing anchors during the week. If there were no absences, then I did whatever the supervisor on duty wanted me to do. Maybe it was watching long news conferences or boring Senate hearings, pulling soundbites from them during the brief periods I was able to concentrate. Occasionally there was the chance to put together a report that had all the elements—a disaster with people's lives in danger, perhaps with a torrent of water and a dramatic rescue caught on videotape. The elements were all there, and I'd do my best to get it on the air as soon as possible. Of course, I could almost be certain it would play maybe twice on the air, then be crushed like a bug, (never to be viewed again), by the incoming news piece from the CNN reporter who was actually on the scene.

Then the fall of 1989 came, and working with CNN Newsource, not only did I get to cover stories like the San Francisco Earthquake, which I detailed earlier, but the Avianca Airliner disaster on Long Island, and Manuel Noriega's capture and return to Miami. It was great exposure for us, and gave 160 CBS, ABC, NBC, and Fox network affiliates their own personal reporter on the scene at a fraction of the cost it would take them to send their own crew there. And since their own networks weren't doing live reports for their local casts, it cemented a relationship with CNN that now involves five hundred-plus affiliates today.

It was a journalist's dream—flying to a breaking story on short notice—but it was in its infancy, and communications were not always tight. In the case of Hurricane Hugo, my flight to Charleston was not okayed until midday on the day the storm struck, so the plane turned around in midflight and returned to Atlanta, given the fact the storm was one hundred miles off the coast. Then I drove an hour to get back home, only to hear the phone ring. It was the vice-president of news, Jon Petrovich, ordering me to go back to the airport and hop on a plane to Norfolk, Virginia, just in case the storm veered northward.

What an exercise in futility. It never even rained a drop in Norfolk.

Meanwhile, my colleagues Chuck Roberts and Charles Zewe were doing a brilliant job, although they were hanging on to anything and everything that was tied down with cement as they gave their reports when the storm's fury plowed ashore.

I watched the storm too—on a little nineteen-inch screen in my Holiday Inn hotel room in Norfolk.

When dawn broke, Peter Arnett was jetting in from the Caribbean where he had covered the storm's destruction there. He called and offered to pick me up in the chartered plane and get me to Charleston, where the major damage was. I called Jon Petrovich, (Petro, to those who were his buddies), and CNN Newsource Manager Jack Womack, who would later replace Petro at Headlines.

The latest news had just come down from the executives. No, I wasn't going to Charleston. I was going to Charlotte, North Carolina, to look around and confirm the reported damage there. A satellite truck would meet me there.

So I drove toward Charlotte like a man possessed. I was going to cover some part of this crazy story. A cat stuck in a tree. No problem. A trash fire in a dumpster. No problem.

I sped into downtown Charlotte, noticing the downed trees and power lines. I called my bosses.

"Gee, Bob, we're really sorry," came the reply. "Really, we are. I guess no one told you the news. The satellite truck broke down. You'll have to drive the rental car back to the Atlanta airport."

I crossed five state lines before I reached the Atlanta airport. Given all the states my exhausted body and muddy car had been through, it cost CNN over a thousand dollars for the car alone . . . in two days. Stardom had its shortcomings.

Many trips, like the one to San Francisco for the 1989 earthquake, fared much better. In mid-1990 CNN Newsource had added on two more experienced reporters, Judy Fortin and Toria Tolley, and my reporting days were over. The next four years found me doing much of what I'd done before: Anchoring, package producing, pulling soundbites, and sitting. I could ask the supervisors for work, but generally they had better things to do than chase down tasks for me to do. If I had an original idea, it became obvious to me I should keep it to myself.

Then October of 1993 rolled around. Jon Petrovich, saw me sitting one day, called me into his office, and said I was to leave the network by January 1994. He didn't think I was working enough. *I agreed with him,* and asked him to use me more in a fill-in role anchoring on the air. I also encouraged him to talk to the supervisors who never used my services.

He was not inclined to take my suggestions. He said he didn't even like the way I smiled all the time. So, I smiled at him. I told him I wasn't going to leave. He begged to differ. I went to see an attorney.

CNN had a rather interesting employment record regarding middle-aged white male anchors from the time of Tom Johnson's arrival as CNN President in May of 1990 to May of 1993. Nine of that endangered species had been tossed or had their contracts not renewed. They were not a happy bunch. Some had trouble getting other anchor jobs. One even wound up sacking groceries in a north Georgia supermarket.

My attorney put the allegations in a big binder and gave out copies to all my fellow malcontents. January of 1994 came and went. My card entry-key still worked. No one said anything, so I just kept coming to work and looking for my name on the schedule. By February I had been assigned to do double shifts on the weekends—7:00 to 3:00 A.M. It was eight hours straight in the anchor chair, with, fortunately, a few fifteen-minute breaks.

Would my voice hold out? We were about to see. Don Harrison had suffered a heart attack doing double shifts on the weekends. I was wondering what health problems, if any, awaited me.

I took the challenge, and almost surprisingly, I grew accustomed to getting four days work done in two, then being put first in line for substitute anchoring on Fridays.

Then January of 1995 rolled around. My yearly review was coming up. I still could not figure out why I hadn't been terminated. Petro didn't do the review—he let one of his lieutenants, Roger Bahre, have the honors.

My review was excellent.

I thought to myself: There's something strange going on here, something I need to figure out.

On the Headline News set, CNN Center, Atlanta, 1994.

I got a pay raise. Bahre acted like nothing had happened until I was walking out of his office.

He suddenly stopped me cold in my tracks.

"Bob, have you seen how many white male anchors are suing their employers these days when they get fired?" I nodded and kept walking. Was he telling me that I was still employed because of the possibility of a lawsuit? I'll probably never know.

My self-satisfaction was short-lived. It ended in October of 1996.

In late 1995, Petro began a full-scale upheaval, aimed at revamping the newsroom's computer and playback equipment, and also aimed at changing the job descriptions and titles of the Headlines staff. The new computers would be able to eventually program more shows on their hard drives, then play stories in different orders just by a few touches of the buttons on the computers.

Whether Petro was intentionally or unintentionally trying for a 50 percent head count reduction among the writers, editors, and producers, he got it whether he wanted it or not. Seventy-six of the 160 editorial employees at Headlines quit. They were not a bunch of malcontents. They were, in many cases, the backbone of the department. Most stayed within the Turner organization. They went upstairs to CNN, across the hall to CNN International, and over to CNN Interactive. But very few went to MSNBC or Fox. My guess would be that 80 percent of them got more money and less strenuous work after they left.

Why, you ask, was there a mass exodus? And perhaps the bigger question—why didn't they leave a long time ago if they could get better money for working fewer hours? The answer to the second question is fairly straightforward—they took pride in taking a bare-bones, sometimes underappreciated network like Headline News, in the shadow of CNN's almost total control of anything live, and putting out a product that was, for the most part, free of glaring editorial or technical errors.

Headline News employees also had to put out more news copy per day than CNN, since CNN's product also included numerous talk shows with only one-minute headlines at the top and bottom of the hour. The fact that the Headline staff was, on average, probably twelve years younger than their seasoned CNN counterparts, and worked bizarre hours as they moved up in the organization, also gave them a strong bond with each other.

Petrovich, in forming the roughly ten advisory committees of staff members at Headline News in 1995, got them to volunteer their time on a weekly basis. They, in turn, gave their input in well-formulated statements suggesting that Headline News should schedule adequate personnel for shifts, integrate the "Avid Airplay" computer system with the formerly all-videotape format, and retrain staff members for multiple jobs. Petro received the recommendations after months of committee meetings—then pitched 90 percent of them right out the window.

Some staff members realized they'd been wasting their free time, and they weren't going to stick around to see which rock Petro was going to steer the ship into. Many writers, editors, and producers simply bailed out, while frustration also grew on the technical side. Petro now had any head count reduction he had ever thought about, plus a whole lot more, and yet the new equipment wasn't doing what he thought it was going to do. It many times froze up in the middle of a show, and the newscasts literally stopped until the backup tape system could get going. Add to that

Petro's attempt to get the editorial people to do technical jobs, and the technical people to suddenly become writers, and the whole project collapsed like a house of cards.

By August of 1996, Petro was on his way to head up the marketing of the new twenty-four-hour CNN Spanish all-news operation in Latin America and South America, and former CNN Newsource boss Jack Womack was brought in to pick up the pieces of a demoralized operation.

I will give Womack credit for stopping the bloodletting. But while Petro had, up until late 1995, kept a hands-off approach to the newsroom, which I thought was a good idea, Jack Womack was a man ready to fight a war. Yet, all his efforts would do him little good as long as CNN kept much of the live breaking stories to itself and kept him on a tight string in a budget-cutting mode. So he was fighting uphill. But perhaps he misinterpreted the signals from management upstairs at CNN.

If the mandate from CNN President Tom Johnson was to slow the ship and straighten the course, Womack had taken that to mean "full speed ahead!"

From August to October of 1996, Womack was a virtual memo factory, and they were flying like the skull and crossbones on the *Jolly Roger*. This was a war he was fighting, and he was throwing the personnel schedules and the job titles into the breach. My turn in the barrel came in the form of two phone calls October 17, 1996.

The first call was from CNN President Tom Johnson, telling me he was cancelling the speech I spent two months preparing for delivery to the American Chamber of Commerce meeting to be held in Hong Kong in just three weeks! I couldn't believe it. Johnson admitted he knew I'd received approval from Roger Bahre, but he was cancelling it for fear of the sensitive issue of the upcoming transfer of power, from Britain to China.

Then I started trying to figure out what had happened. It turned out that my calls to the CNN Hong Kong Bureau to invite them to come hear my speech proved to be my undoing. I suspected, (and later got corroboration from CNN public relations director Steve Haworth), that someone in that bureau had called Johnson behind my back, and after laying out their argument against my trip, got Johnson's support.

I do understand the reasoning, but it was an embarrassment not only to the sponsors of my speech, but to the American Chamber which had sold three hundred tickets for the event. It also gave CNN a black eye. I think the considerable research I had done on Hong Kong and the view of the press from many sides would have made CNN proud. But this latest little dose of reality told me that I had better get approval from the absolute top of CNN before venturing into any speech where what I was saying might be dissected and scrutinized, and where my appearance might not get a friendly reception from the local CNN bureau.

Interestingly enough, CNN Hong Kong bureau chief Mike Chinoy addressed the American Chamber the following month.

Later that same day in October of 1996, there was another bulletin handed to me by management. And the news was about as pleasant as going to a party at a house where the couple entertaining you has just had a fight. Whether it was just a coincidence, I'll probably never know, but Jack Womack was replacing me on the 7:00 P.M. to 11:00 P.M. part of my double shift, leaving me with the late night, 11:00 P.M. to 3:00 A.M. slot Saturday and Sunday nights.

I was stunned. Ten years of working 7:00 P.M. to 11:00 P.M. was now a memory. It was package-producing time again, and I felt unwanted.

I asked Jack if the ratings for the shows were bad? *No.* Any problem with my performance on the air? Again—*No* was the reply. He said he just wanted more variety on Saturday and Sunday nights.

He also made sure I realized that he had twenty qualified people a week coming to him, wanting to be on the air at Headline News. As he said in a memo to me, I ought to feel lucky just to work there. Funny, but suddenly I didn't.

Ironically, almost a year later in September of 1997, not long after ABC veteran Rick Kaplan was handed the CNN presidency as Tom Johnson moved up to the title of chairman of CNN, longtime CNN executive Bob Furnad was appointed to the new title of president of CNN Headline News, with Womack keeping the title of executive vice-president, but reporting to Furnad.

Just as quickly, Patrice Formby, the female anchor who was chosen to replace me in that prime-time 7:00 P.M. to 11:00 P.M. slot Saturday and Sunday nights was being bumped off the shift, and left of her own accord in October of 1997. Suddenly, the only place where there was more *bumping* going in was in the Super Bowl.

In my final months at Headline News, there were times when I felt like author Scott Adams's cartoon character, Dilbert. All I needed was a cubicle, perhaps shrunken down to four feet by four feet to reflect my new status. On those frequent package-producing days I felt like a timer on the railroad. If I went to CNN upstairs, I had to enter the time in the computer.

Headed to lunch. Enter the time in the computer.

Mother called. Enter the time in the computer.

In February of 1997 I went to speak to the Oklahoma Broadcaster's Association and visit my mother in Tulsa for Valentine's Day. I called Atlanta to check my messages, and found that Womack was curious why I was taking my earned six weeks of vacation, three days at a time, Wednesday through Friday, when he wanted to keep his eye on me. He wanted to know what I was speaking about, and how much I was getting paid.

By now I was looking around for some stealth camera, smaller than a microbe, farther away than a football field, snapping pictures of me through a window in a small room where I was sitting.

Ironically, the room I was sitting in was an attorney's office. The attorney and I were discussing my mother's business affairs, but I thought I'd better call Womack back immediately. He wasn't in, so I left him the attorney's number . . . which he never called.

Back at my hotel four hours later, I received a fax from Jack: "We understand about your mother. We're behind you all the way. Take all the time you need."

What an interesting study in human psychology. Mr. Hyde, please meet Dr. Jekyll. I appreciated his empathy, real or imagined.

That lasted about four weeks.

In April of '97, Jack wanted to know who I had done corporate video work for. He was concerned over a call by one person to the New York CNN Bureau after viewing a private showing of a promotional tape I had done. I told him I'd get to the bottom of it, but I also told him that if I was to be singled out for doing any training and promotion videos, all other anchors would have to be asked to reveal theirs as well.

As far as I was concerned, Jack was revving up his engine over nothing, since I didn't do commercials, never interviewed corporate clients on the air, and never dealt with anyone not affiliated with a blue-chip organization.

Perhaps Jack was feeling pressure from management above him, but it seemed to me that if I was required to list all my outside video work, any prohibition would be clearly stated and signed by both parties in my *contract*—and mine hadn't been renewed since my little picnic in Petro's office in late 1993. Had I not been so dismayed after that encounter, I probably would have tried to protect my future by pursuing opportunities outside Headline News. But Jack had found an issue he could hold over me indefinitely.

It was time to let go. No more cubicle police. No more jumping through hoops like a trained chi-hua-hua.

May 7, 1997, I left, and on May 8 I was planning my schedule for several corporate videos and looking ahead to several speaking engagements.

Jack was going to be happier, and could replace me with people costing less than half of what he was paying me. I was embarking on a new, positive relationship with many firms. I was now working for myself for the first time in my thirty-year career, rising or falling on what I did as an on-camera and voice-over talent, in a field that requires skills quite similar to those I used in broadcasting the news. I was also stepping up my speaking engagements, and was fortunate to be admitted as a member of a group I could learn a lot from—the National Speakers Association.

At the same time, I was not going to shut the door on future broadcasting opportunities. I had enjoyed the camaraderie of working alongside the journalists, like those I found at Headline News—a true team effort.

CHAPTER FIFTEEN

The Long and Winding Road

EVERY NOW AND THEN I'LL BE SPEAKING TO A GROUP and realize that I either have my pages out of order, I'm missing a page, or . . . in the most embarrassing case, I start coughing uncontrollably, have to sit down, and ask for a glass of water. That was the worst, until my speech to five Rotary Clubs at a dinner in Bryan, Ohio.

I had taken a whirlwind tour of the Etch-A-Sketch factory, the local paper, a heat exchanger factory, a nearby high school, and finally, the Spangler Candy Company prior to speaking that evening.

The Spangler Candy Company was my last stop on the tour. Curtis suckers and Dum-Dums were being made by a giant mixmaster-looking device that stirred huge amounts of gooey sugar in large vats.

I remember tromping around on the sugar-coated floor for over an hour before going back to my hotel room to rest up for a few minutes before the speech.

I sat on the edge of the bed, still clothed in my black suit which had turned an ashen color from all the powdered sugar I had stepped in on the factory floor. I leaned back for just a moment's rest.

I fell asleep, waking up just five minutes before the speech.

What to do! I sat up at the foot of the bed and straightened my tie, but as I stood up, I nearly fell over on my face.

My shoes, coated with that sugary syrup that had now hardened, were stuck to the floor. It was like Super-Glue! I untied my shoes, and dashed out of the room in my stocking feet, passing many of the arriving audience members as I rushed down the hall to the front desk.

"Do you have any carpet shears or scissors?" I pleaded.

"No we don't, Mr. Losure," she replied.

I was still in my panic mode, but trying to think.

"Do you have a letter opener, then?" I inquired.

She had that. Of course, by the look in her eye, she was a little nervous about what I was up to.

I got back to my room, worked the letter opener around the edges of the shoes, and finally freed them. I stood up and felt like I had Super-Glue and half-an-inch of carpeting stuck firmly to my shoes. I looked like the Frankenstein monster. It was kind of like I was wearing a pair of black platform-heeled men's disco-dancing shoes from the '70s. All I needed were some tight bell-bottoms.

Ironically, few in the audience knew who I was anyway since their local cable system didn't carry Headline News. I guess I should feel fortunate that the Holiday Inn staff had a letter opener that I could borrow—at least I didn't have to do the speech in my stocking feet.

Air Force Captain Scott O'Grady with me in Atlanta, 1997.

It is one thing to talk about being independent, working for yourself and hustling up your own business. It is another to actually go out and do it and be successful at it after so many years of getting that paycheck like clockwork every couple of weeks. Then, there are life's real struggles. U.S. Air Force fighter pilot, Captain Scott O'Grady, whose dramatic rescue after being shot down over Bosnia in 1995 led to his book *Return with Honor*, has been a great friend to

Astronaut Alan Shepard
with me at Aviation
Challenge at the
U.S. Space Camp in 1991.

me before and after my separation from Headline News. His story about hiding from Serbian troops for six days in the mountains of Bosnia and being found and rescued by U.S. Marines has never stopped fascinating me.

I was emceeing a dinner in Atlanta in 1995, and Scott and I were talking about the do's and don'ts of book tours, when a banquet server appeared with our salads. Scott leaned over to the young woman and asked if he could just have a bowl of seasonal strawberries and blueberries. She rushed to get the berries and I asked Scott why he didn't want his salad. He said, "I just can't eat tossed salads anymore. They remind me of all that green stuff I picked off the ground and ate while I was being chased around the countryside in Bosnia."

In 1991, I met another true hero, America's first astronaut, Alan Shepard. He faced and conquered the unknown dangers of space in 1961. I met him in Huntsville, Alabama, at a fun gathering of about thirty-five media people from radio, television stations, and newspapers across the country. We were there to experience NASA's U.S. Space Camp and their new program, Aviation Challenge.

It wasn't long before I proved that as far as being an astronaut or a jet pilot, I'll never have "the right stuff." We media types split up into teams to experience the feeling of being a NASA ground control team and the crew of the space shuttle. I served as the commander of my simulated shuttle mission in a realistic mock-up, and re-entered the earth's atmosphere for a successful landing.

Dangling periously above the water as I learn to parachute.

Mission Control called me to inquire about the whereabouts of two of my astronauts who were on board the craft. I turned around and looked back at the open payload bay behind me.

Oops! I had inadvertently left two of my crew members in an open payload bay, re-entered the earth's atmosphere at eighteen-thousand miles an hour with the heat building to three-thousand degrees. If it had been the real thing, I would have had two crispy critters on my hands.

Then there were other challenges like traveling seven miles an hour at a ten degree angle down a long wire into the manmade lake at the Aviation Challenge site, simulating a parachute drop. At the end of the wire, I unlocked myself, swam to a raft, paddled the raft over to a hoist with a simulated helicopter above, and pulled up in a mock rescue. Everything went well. But I couldn't leave well enough alone. I showed up for the final simulated Top Gun competition, curious about how the F/A-18, F-15, and F-14 jet simulators worked. Each simulator had altimeter readings, a radar screen, a visual screen, missile and machine gun controls, and of course the joystick to steer the thing. I watched the preliminaries in awe, wondering how my fellow Aviation Challenge members could have such dexterity with what resembled a video game. So the five finalists for the Top Gun award climbed into their simu-lated jet fighters. A sixth simulator wasn't being used, so I was goaded into climbing into the cockpit to be the first sacrificial lamb to be shot down.

I called one of the instructors over just to help me get the plane off the ground. My colleagues already had their planes in the air and were preparing to fly by each other at an altitude of ten-thousand feet, and just like Snoopy and the Red Baron, the "dogfight" would begin.

I was still trying to get my plane off the ground.

Suddenly, there was the sound of simulated missiles and machine guns being fired. I revved up my engine and pulled back on the joystick. I was airborne.

There was only one problem. I couldn't figure out how to bring the nose of the jet back level. So I kept gaining altitude, flying so high that if I were a pilot, I'd begin leaving earth's atmosphere. The other jets took a few shots at me, but I was so far out of range of their missiles that I was disappearing from their radar scopes!

Slowly, I gained some control of my craft about the time I was seemingly halfway to the moon, but back on earth the dogfight had taken its toll. The two remaining aircraft crashed trying to overmanuever each other.

I was still clowning around in outer space, but I was declared the winner, having never fired a shot. Alan Shepard presented me with the Top Gun Award the next day, along with a replica of the jacket Tom Cruise wore in the movie of the same name. I had proved that once in a great while, luck wins out over skill and knowledge. I figure I would be passing the planet Neptune right now if the dogfight hadn't been declared over.

Before leaving CNN, I had spent three years getting ready for the day when *I* could decide what holidays *I* would take off, when I could decide which projects I wanted to take on. The alternative, moving around the country from one anchor chair to another, was not as alluring to me as it had been fifteen years before.

The list of corporations who want me to speak on their behalf, either on videotape, or to their audience directly, is still growing. Firms like United Consumers Club, Gulliver-Ritchie Associates, Bell South, United Parcel Service, Georgia Power, Siemens Corporation, Bayer Pharmaceutical, Nationwide Auto, Wal-Mart, Lutheran Bible Translators and CSX Railroad have been exceedingly kind to give me work.

In 1997, I was invited to Burt Reynolds Ranch in Jupiter, Florida. We were shooting a pilot for a series on wildlife rangers and their duties from hunting down poachers to taking care of endangered species. I was the host, doing both on-camera and narrative parts in what was part "Wild Kingdom" and part re-enactment, a little like "Real Stories of the Highway Patrol." Burt was out in Los Angeles publicizing the movie *Boogie Nights,* but I did get to talk to his father, who at the golden young age of ninety patrols the 160-acre ranch and nature preserve on a golf cart, checking on the many deer, horses, and wild birds.

Burt has quite a collection of old movie sets, including the Long Branch Saloon from the long-running "Gunsmoke," one of the first series he worked in (he was cast as Dodge City's blacksmith). He even had the yacht set from *Striptease,* in which he costarred with Demi Moore. Sadly, Burt's financial woes prior to his renewed star status as recent acting award nominee may force him to sell much of that, including the land.

Part of the videotape pilot involved rolling up my pants legs and standing in a swamp, which certainly encouraged me to do my standups right the first time. I did several other portions of the pilot in front of the gas station used in *Smokey and the Bandit II.* It wasn't just a facade either. About midway through the shooting, an eighty-year-old employee of the ranch showed up, unlocked the gas station's door, and showed us the inside of the station, converted to a log home complete with a four-poster bed.

I have been fortunate over the last couple of years to emcee events for the United States Junior Chamber of Commerce and JCI, their huge international group. It has taken me from Washington, D.C., to Pusan, South Korea. I was translated into fourteen languages at the Pusan event in 1996, but I'm not sure to this day whether I was translated word for word. You see, I would talk for about a minute, introducing various dignitaries from the more than 140 countries represented. Then my Korean translator next to me at the podium, a lovely young anchorwoman from Seoul, would translate it all in less than fifteen seconds. She would then turn to me, smile, and wait for the look of surprise on my face. Was she giving an edited version to the audience?

The U.S. Junior Chamber of Commerce Ten Outstanding Young Americans awards in Washington, D.C., January 1998.

This went on for about five rounds of translation, then I deviated from the script . . . intentionally, just to see what she would do. I started talking about how much I liked being in Korea, and how warm and friendly my Korean co-emcee at the podium had been to me. It took all of fifteen seconds.

It took her over a minute to translate. Then it got a thunderous ovation, followed by some side-splitting laughter from the mainly Korean audience among the nine thousand people in attendance.

For all I know, she may have been playfully saying, "The crazy American anchorman is one of the biggest fools I've ever met. Please humor him by applauding, then laughing, so he'll think he's a big shot."

Maybe it's good I never found out the exact translation.

CHAPTER SIXTEEN

"60 Minutes" from the Other Side of the Microphone

THERE I WAS EYEBALL TO EYEBALL WITH ED BRADLEY OF "60 Minutes," and it wasn't a dream. It was November 6, 1997, in a small studio on the ninth floor of the CBS building at 555 West Fifty-seventh Street in New York City. What on earth was I doing in the jaws of a tiger like Ed Bradley on a show that week-in and week-out chews up guests into little, hardly discernible pieces?

The saga began in October of 1995 when I decided to make an investment, that for me, was a healthy sum of money—$14,500 to be exact. I was in the offices of Atlanta document and rare gem specialist Tom Cloud, President of Cloud and Associates and National Historical Autographs. Sitting with us was a close personal friend, E. A. Gresham, who had told me of the sale Cloud was conducting. In front of us were several pieces of paper, several notecards, and a magazine, perhaps sixty or seventy documents in all. Together, these documents would be sold over the next month for over two million dollars. In all, 280 of the 324 documents, totaling seven hundred pages, were sold privately between 1993 and 1996 for over six million dollars. Four billionaires, including *Forbes* magazine magnate and former presidential candidate Steve Forbes, had invested. Tom Cloud was the third biggest investor in terms of money spent, so he had a real stake in making sure the documents were authentic. I could easily be classified as a small investor.

Tom Cloud thumbed through the note cards, pausing to read the cryptic typewritten messages, many of them quotes from Sir Arthur Conan Doyle's Sherlock Holmes mysteries, then flipping the card over to read the barely legible scrawling on the other side, always with the name *Jack* at the bottom.

As Cloud showed me the documents, I was fascinated by the stories behind them. They had belonged to Lawrence X. Cusack Sr., who is believed to have been a long-standing friend of President John F. (Jack) Kennedy and his father, Joe Kennedy. It was Cusack who allegedly helped pave the way with the New York archdiocese for Kennedy's annulment of his secret first marriage in 1947 to Durie Malcolm. Kennedy, of course, would later marry Jacqueline Bouvier in 1953.

For many years, Cusack, from his office in New York, would correspond with President Kennedy by use of couriers who made private deliveries of note cards and letters. Cusack died in 1985, and his son, Lawrence (Lex) Cusack III found the Kennedy documents in four different locations between 1987 and 1993, and showed them to another collectibles dealer and authenticator of documents, John Reznikoff, who then solicited Cloud for the sale.

Among the documents were typewritten and handwritten notes from Marilyn Monroe to President Kennedy, promising to keep their hidden relationship a secret.

Another typed document showed a $600 thousand payoff from Joseph Kennedy, President Kennedy's father, to Monroe. It was the beginning of several payments to again assure her secrecy. There were also well over a hundred of the index cards with the curious Sherlock Holmes quotes on one side, and President Kennedy's brief ten-to-fifteen-word handwritten messages on the other. It appeared that Kennedy was worried that FBI head J. Edgar Hoover knew of the payoffs to Monroe, as well as Kennedy's secret relationship with her.

One of the cards read, on the typewritten side:

His Last Bow

". . . On these his eager, questioning eyes
were fixed, and I saw on his keen, alert
face that tightening of the lips, that quiver
of the nostrils, and concentration of the
heavy, tufted brows which I knew so well."

On the reverse side of the card was the written message:

Larry—
Yes
More of this
I can not take

Attack from
Hoover is too
much—
Jack

I bought the card on the spot for $10,750. A photocopy of the document had handwriting on the side in red ink from Robert L. White, who holds the largest private collection of Kennedy memorabilia outside the Kennedy family itself, in the world. It read:

May 1, 1995
To Whom It May Concern:
The above copied handwriting and signature
"Jack" on the card is in my opinion that of
John F. Kennedy.
Robert L. White

The other item I bought was a *TIME* magazine dated October 10, 1960, just before Kennedy's victory in the November election. It had Jack's brother and campaign manager Bobby Kennedy on the cover, and a short message written in the upper third of the cover from Jack Kennedy to Larry Cusack, thanking him for his help through some trying times. It too was authenticated by Robert L. White.

I paid $3,750 for the magazine, one of only three magazines that Kennedy is believed to have written on.

I left the note card and the magazine in Cloud's possession for storage in a vault. I could just imagine myself in my car, driving down the road with my new purchase, rolling down the window, and watching as the note card and magazine flew out the window onto a busy Atlanta highway, with an eighteen-wheeler putting its own personal stamp of approval on them.

TIME magazine, October 10, 1960.

I could then visualize driving back to Cloud's office—with the only Jack Kennedy documents in the world with tread marks on them.

The excitement of the documents was enhanced by the fact that Pulitzer-prize-winning author Seymour Hersh was researching a book to be called *The Dark Side of Camelot,* and much of his information was coming from the 324 documents.

They detailed Jack Kennedy's fear of being blackmailed by J. Edgar Hoover over his liaisons with several women in the White House while wife Jackie was away. The documents' information was corroborated by first-time interviews with four of the former Secret Service agents who knew of Kennedy's sexual liaisons with other women, including Judith Campbell Exner. The book also explored alleged voting irregularities masterminded by Chicago mob boss Sam Giancana that handed Kennedy his narrow victory in the 1960 election.

Hersh figured that with the substantial written and typed evidence of payoffs not only to Marilyn Monroe, but to First Lady Jackie Kennedy, Hersh would be raising not only the value of the Cusack/Cloud documents, but also the interest in his novel. Hersh, Cusack, and Cloud also collaborated with Lancer Productions, which was doing a two-hour documentary for ABC on the book and the new documents. It was to be narrated by ABC anchor Peter Jennings and telecast in November of 1997 in primetime. An auction of the documents was to follow in December 1997 under the auspices of Empire Auction in New York. Even the rights to a movie were being talked about in glowing terms.

But just as the glory days of Camelot in the Kennedy White House ended abruptly, so the end came abruptly to the dreams of Lex and Jennifer Cusack, Tom and Polly Cloud, and the 140 other investors who had put so much hope in the documents.

The party ended September 25, 1997, when Lex Cusack, who had been working side by side ABC for months in preparation for the documentary, suddenly found himself under interrogation. After sitting under hot television lights for nearly an hour, waiting for his crowning moment—an interview by Peter Jennings—the door to the hotel room in New York flew open. Jennings Superman persona had turned to Darth Vader in what is known in the business as an ambush interview. Cusack's enthusiasm to be part of a documentary was about to vanish. Jennings was in the mood for some straight answers for ABC's "20/20" investigative program. He began grilling an already perspiring Cusack on the documents. He told Cusack that ABC had hired two forensics experts, Gerald Richards and Linda Hart, who were familiar with the study of typewritten documents, but not written documents. They said the documents they examined were not genuine.

Cusack refused to budge. He was adamant that he had not falsified any documents nor had he instructed others to falsify them. Yet the damage was done.

ABC's two experts, neither of whom had ever studied John F. Kennedy's handwriting, concentrated on six typewritten documents. Twenty-four handwritten documents that the two experts were also given were never discussed on the show, perhaps because Jerry Richards and Linda Hart did notice that on the two Monroe typewritten documents, a lift-off ribbon to correct mistakes appeared to have been used. But Richards and Hart contended that typewriters on which the documents were typed in the late '50s and early '60s did not have the capability of using a correcting ribbon. Cloud and Cusack later found lift-off ribbon advertised in the *Office Magazine*, published 1958–1962, the period in question. Later, Cloud and Cusack would try to point out the irregularities in typewriters of that period, where a key frequently made a lift-off ribbon type of impression by striking a page with a flicking motion, without hitting the inked ribbon.

From the ABC "20/20" interview that Jennings did, newspapers picked up on the story of a supposed massive hoax. A Manhattan grand jury was impaneled to look at who might be guilty if indeed the documents had been forged, and by whom. The grand jury subpoenaed 110 of the 324 documents, so any attempt at re-authentication of those would have to wait.

Meanwhile, over at CBS, "60 Minutes" producers Jonathan Wells and Michael Radutzky also sensed that the story had scandal written all over it, given the fact that ABC and Seymour Hersh had backed completely away from supporting the documents and from even talking to Cusack and Cloud after the ABC "20/20" special.

Cusack's dream of keeping one of his homes in Connecticut was about to evaporate. Cloud's solid reputation as a dealer in collectibles and precious gems was being tarnished. Experts like Robert L. White, who had seen hundreds of authentic and mechanized auto-pen signatures of Jack Kennedy over the years, suddenly were hedging on whether they could definitively say the documents were real. I, of course, watched with heightened interest and listened.

To add to the dilemma, renowned handwriting authenticator Charles Hamilton, who had put his authentication on the documents that he looked at in 1995, died in January of 1997. His widow, Diane, herself a signature expert, came forth to be interviewed by "60 Minutes."

The current dean of authenticators, noted signature expert Bob Batchelder, made himself available to "60 Minutes," but was never asked to give his opinion or be interviewed in New York. He had authenticated three of the documents previously for Tom Cloud.

When "60 Minutes" Producer Jonathan Wells called me November 1, he was adamant that "60 Minutes" wanted to get "the other side" of the authentication controversy, and asked if I would come to New York to be interviewed. I immediately volunteered. I believed in Tom Cloud's veracity then and today, and I knew he could use some support.

I realized that it could be the same kind of interview that I had coached executives about dealing with for years. It is known as ambush journalism, where you find yourself approached by a reporter in a public place unprepared, or you come into a studio to be interviewed for something you've been told will be have a positive slant, and the interviewer has a set of embarrassing questions all lined up.

I did expect "60 Minutes" to have several experts who, like the ABC authenticators, would also brush aside the documents as a

Bob and CBS Correspondent
Ed Bradley at "60 Minutes"
studios in Manhattan, 1997.

hoax. That had been the thread of every news story I had read, and the story would not be the kind of controversy that "60 Minutes" would want if everything checked out perfectly.

It was 10:00 A.M., Thursday, November 6, 1997. On the ninth floor of the CBS building, crews were putting their last-minute touches on the lighting along with the three cameras used in the shoot. Ed Bradley strolled in, smiling.

"I already know who you are," he said, referring to me. We shook hands.

He then turned his attention to Gary Vick, a financial consultant in Albuquerque, who was the other investor to come forth and stand behind his friend of many years, Tom Cloud.

Bradley sat down scarcely two feet from Gary and me. Two cameras were just inches from Bradley's left shoulder and two feet from our faces. Another camera was over my right shoulder, eighteen inches away, shooting Bradley's questions and reaction.

For some strange reason, I felt comfortable. I wanted to get the point across that an independent group of perhaps half-a-dozen handwriting analysts with experience in looking at Kennedy's and Monroe's handwriting should be chosen. They in turn would look at perhaps a hundred of the documents to make some definitive comparisons.

For impartiality's sake, I wanted Cloud and ABC to agree to each pay half the cost of the analysis. If they couldn't agree, perhaps a private foundation not connected to either side could step in and pay for it, or as a last resort, the experts would donate their time.

Bradley began the interview by asking basic questions concerning the date when Gary and I first saw the documents, which documents we purchased, and our relationship with Cloud.

About eight minutes into the interview, Bradley paused, put his reading glasses on, and glanced down at his legal-size pad with questions written on it.

"Gentlemen, our own expert, Duayne Dillon, took a look at many of the documents. He has looked at a total of twenty-six of them, and his findings are that they are . . . how do I put this . . . indeed, a hoax. What do you have to say?"

I sat perfectly still. My facial expression remained neutral. I wasn't pleased. I wasn't sad. I wasn't even surprised.

I told Bradley of my feeling that the documents needed to be independently examined by someone who wasn't getting paid for their answers, and explained the kind of process that I thought would clear up a lot of the debate.

Bradley again tried to get a reaction, this time on issue of re-authentication.

"You know, we have talked to these experts that Mr. Cloud listed as authenticators of these documents. We found that nine of the twelve experts have refused to re-authenticate. I find that a little strange. What do you say to that?"

I expanded on my previous answer, wondering aloud that if the Declaration of Independence and the Constitution were to be examined for authenticity, would they meet all the criteria by a panel of examiners for authentication, if they didn't know where they came from?

I doubt that Ed Bradley was impressed with my effort to turn the interview around and ask him questions.

Bradley is a very smooth interviewer whose understated tone has been known to lull more than one interviewee into divulging the truth that few other interviewers could get to. Bradley, peering over the top of his glasses as his head angled downward, asked another version of his question about the lack of re-authentication by most of Cloud's experts, but Gary and I kept giving him the same answers. I made the presumption, which later proved to be correct, that the original authenticators had not even had the time to come back and look at the documents, and most of the documents were still being shuffled back and forth to the Manhattan grand jury.

Bradley had been unsuccessful in his attempt to draw out of us the kind of worried looks, sweat, or loud protestations that reporters look for. So the interview ended about eighteen minutes after it began, and Bradley prepared to interview handwriting expert Diane Brooks Hamilton, who was on Cloud's side of the authentication issue.

On Friday, November 21, 1997, Cloud and Cusack each filed $50 million defamation of character lawsuits against ABC, Peter Jennings, Roone Arledge, Seymour Hersh, and several others. They felt they had been betrayed by ABC after working so closely with the network from 1995 to 1997.

Sunday night, November 23, after a week's delay, the JFK segment aired on "60 Minutes." The report explained the history of the Kennedy and Monroe documents, and introduced the handwriting expert hired by "60 Minutes," Duayne Dillon. He was shown going over ten of the documents with a microscope. He said that all of them appeared to have flaws, with the capital letter G made differently than some known Kennedy documents, and some words with letters disjointed, unlike Kennedy's handwriting. Later, after the report aired, he admitted that he had not studied Kennedy's and Monroe's handwriting previously, and had seen only a few samples.

The "60 Minutes" report appeared to break little new ground. A wider variety of experts should have been brought in to look at so many different styles of handwriting and typing. Even the one handwriting expert from the Cloud-Cusack side that "60 Minutes" interviewed on camera, Diane Brooks Hamilton, saw all her comments end up on the cutting-room floor.

When the furor over the documents originally surfaced in September, Cloud sent two of the Kennedy documents that he had to the FBI to be examined at Raleigh, North Carolina, for paper and ink analysis. The tests showed the documents were from the period of the late '50s or early '60s. Yet that information was never put on the "60 Minutes" program.

Bradley's interview of Gary Vick and me was edited down to less than a minute for the show. I don't argue with that, but I do believe the "60 Minutes" team had its mind firmly made up before the thirteen-minute segment was even shot, and we became the pieces to be placed in the predesignated slots.

The truth, given the conflicting analysis by experts, may never be definitively known, though I believe the majority of the documents are real. Some of the documents could be fakes, and in fact the typewritten documents relating to Marilyn Monroe, of which there are only half-a-dozen, have been by far the most scrutinized and most maligned. The picture became even more muddied when Robert L. White, the largest non-Kennedy holder of Kennedy memorabilia in the world, unexplainedly told the "60 Minutes" crew that his authentication of the documents was not really valid because he's not an expert in the field. The truth is that White was such an expert that Cloud, who had seen hundreds of Kennedy signatures over the years, deferred to White for his expertise in the area. White's own letterhead states that he is a handwriting expert.

Why did White change his story? Why did a Pulitzer-prize-winning author like Seymour Hersh believe in the authenticity one day, then the next day completely throw up his hands in dismay after two ABC experts looked at probably no more than 6 of the 324 documents?

Perhaps they'll reveal their reasons in court. They, along with others including Ed Bradley, CBS, and "60 Minutes" are being sued by 100 of the 140 original investors.

Ironically, even if ABC and/or CBS settle out of court, and those who invested are compensated, the damage from a massive media condemnation of the documents, based primarily on three people paid by CBS and ABC to look at fewer than 5 percent of the documents, most likely will never be undone.

An even darker cloud engulfed the documents in March of '98 with the arrest of Lex Cusack at his Fairfield, Connecticut, home.

He was charged with mail fraud, and accused of masterminding what would be one of the most sensational forgeries in history. Still, Cusack refused to plead guilty. He instead hired a legal team to challenge the government's case.

The federal government is likely to show Cusack's notepads where it appeared he was trying to duplicate the signatures of President George Washington and other presidents, though it's not known whether John F. Kennedy was among them. The government is also likely to construct its case around ZIP codes used on envelopes from the Cusack collection in the years just before they were initiated, and rely on the authenticators claiming to be experts on the ABC and CBS exposés.

A couple of questions will also be thrown in the lap of any jury impaneled to hear the Cusack case. Were some of the most closely scrutinized and maligned documents, the typewritten ones about a hush agreement between Marilyn Monroe, Jack Kennedy, and patriarch Joe Kennedy forged within the years immediately following their deaths in the '60s? And, how about the more than 250 handwritten documents with 1960s ink, aged paper, and authentic watermarks appearing on official United States stationery? It's an authentication case that could keep Hercule Poirot or Sherlock Holmes up late at night, and unless Cusack unexpectedly admits guilt, it could be a case talked about well into the twenty-first century.

CHAPTER SEVENTEEN

You're Welcome to My Opinion

THOSE OF US WHO HAVE ASPIRED TO BE BROADCAST journalists, delivering the news in a straight-forward manner in hopes that the news itself would be the star, may have been fooling ourselves to a certain extent. It is our own personal style, our longevity in front of an audience, our ability to be seen as real people with a charming personality on the air, that most often influences the ratings. It doesn't hurt to have "Oprah" as your lead-in show either, but however you achieve your ratings, it translates to a network or station's bottom line.

Sometimes the highly stylized look we bring to the anchor desk can be a great source of material for comedians.

I was watching NBC's "Later with Greg Kinnear" one night in early 1995 when I claimed not the fifteen minutes of fame that Andy Warhol promised us, but a few seconds at least.

Kinnear, who built a reputation as a satirist on E! Entertainment's "Talk Soup," had former "Saturday Night Live" star Phil Hartman on the show. I was watching as Kinnear asked Hartman how he developed his character of the wacko passive-aggressive radio news anchorman Bill McNeil, for the TV show, "NewsRadio."

Hartman said the character was "related in large part to the guy in the anchor chair today who has extrapolated the style of the classic newscasters of the past like Walter Cronkite and Edward R. Murrow, and all those foreign correspondents during World War II."

Then the conversation took an unexpected turn, as Kinnear began heading toward the punch line.

"Phil, did you ever follow, when you were looking into doing this show, any news broadcasters . . . because they do have a real style. . . ."

"Oh yeah, Greg. There seems to be a cookie-cutter American broadcaster. . . ."

"CNN is the best place to . . ."

"Yes, you're absolutely right. . . ."

Then Kinnear, his voice rising then falling at the end of the name, exclaimed:

"I'm
  Bob
    Lowww . . .
      zhhure. . . ."

Hartman, his voice deepening, his chin dropping, his left arm resting on the desk in a true anchorman pose, did Kinnear one better.

"Bob Losure with the latest news! This just in!"

I stared at the screen in disbelief. My 15 seconds of fame was complete.

Kinnear and Hartman then moved on to satirize Liz Taylor, then Bill Clinton, so I was off the hook. Whether I was being satirized or complimented actually didn't matter. Kinnear's show was probably being seen by six times the normal Headline News audience, and just as importantly, they pronounced my name correctly.

Maybe that cookie-cutter look that Phil Hartman talked about applies not only to anchors but to news sets, promos, crime stories, and just about everything else that looks like it has the same DNA. Behind that look is the driving force of the big consulting firms like Frank Magid, Audience Research & Development, Broadcast Image Consultants, McHugh and Hoffman, and about four or five others. They grabbed control of the research contracts, then the actual on-air look of the station groups about twenty years ago, and they've never let go. And they've cloned what works for their biggest clients.

They can also show you thousands of examples of ratings improvements in their client stations' ratings books over the years.

The old cliché that "if it bleeds, it leads" was never truer than in today's local news. The school board meeting on a change in school boundaries, the Department of Corrections meeting to release inmates on early parole to ease overcrowding, and the platforms that the county commission candidates are running on—all too often go uncovered by stations unless there's a hint that a fistfight may break out.

I realize that it takes longer to craft a carefully woven story that tugs at your emotions or gets you out of a comfortable chair to take action, so it's not surprising that the easier, get-it-done-in-one-day mentality of covering only violence generally wins out in news. I think daily newspapers are an excellent way to keep up on the news for those people who will take the time to read them front to back. Still, over 70 percent of Americans get most of their news only from television. So it's no wonder we are seeing more people alienated from the election process and the volunteer groups in their communities. They simply don't feel like they're a part of it.

While the Federal Communications Commission, now with hundreds of cable channels to monitor, long ago cut way back on trying to see whether a station serves its community, there has to be a way to cover those stories that affect the whole community, just not those that titillate because a baby was kidnapped in a custody fight. The way to do that is by thoughtful, enterprising journalism, perhaps with a team of reporters. Perhaps with prime-time one-hour specials. WFAA in Dallas has had success with that. Yet it costs money, a lot of it, to keep reporters on one story day after day. Since stations can make a lot more money by sending a reporter out at 11:00 P.M. to stand in the rain and talk about a new crime each night, it is not surprising that the bottom line has won out.

I do see where the tabloid approach to promos for news shows will finally reach a saturation point. So too will the accent on live reports with the reporter standing in front of a courthouse or a previously rain-swollen creek, just for the effect of being live at 11:00 at night. The viewers won't have time in their increasingly busy lives to watch a reporter drone on with absolutely nothing going on in the scene behind them.

Local stations are going to have to change their news focus to survive in the twenty-first century. Audiences are being eroded rapidly by narrow niche programming in areas of documentaries, sports, pay-per-view movies, and by choices on the Internet. The Internet, as it expands into real-time video and audio, and its video becomes larger and more bold in its clarity, will soon be television quality. Add to that the amount of text and still photo information readily accessible and the Internet becomes an integral part of most Americans' lives within five years.

Documentaries on channels like A & E, The Learning Channel, the Discovery Channel, the History Channel, and others are forcing the networks to do more investigative work. ABC's "Nightline" with Ted Koppel is a great example. Thoughtful stories that may take weeks to prepare are giving us more than just so-called talking heads on the subject of the day.

Even VH-1, known for its nonstop music videos, contracted independently to have producers take multiple hours to look behind the facade of rock stars of today, to get to their humanity, their suffering, their triumphs. The result in December of '97 was more than a dozen specials, all with a high-degree of insight.

The kind of long-form programming like VH-1 is doing is going to force local stations to eventually add to the current staple of nonstop muggings, murders, and kidnappings. That's not to say that coverage of these tragedies is going to be abandoned, but it means expanded newscasts and more news specials to give people a real sense of the fascinating discoveries in medicine, or trends in economics in their own communities—something they can't get in a fifteen-second soundbite.

Over the next few years, web sites on the Internet will contain lists of perhaps twenty local stories from each station, all listed and briefly described, so the viewer on the combination computer/television of the twenty-first century will be able to pick and choose what interests them most. I am concerned with the trend of letting viewers decide which stories they want to see on the air. On the Internet, that's fine. But since you can't currently download those stories from the TV screen, you may want to see a newsworthy story that gets zapped in favor of something far more titillating— like strippers on stage at a local club, or the latest movie sensation of the moment putting his/her hands in cement at Mann's Theatre in Los Angeles. If that's the way a station's journalistic reputation is to be compromised, just bring on Jerry Springer and forget about choices and journalism.

I don't mind stations' attempts to break the mold. I've often wondered why almost every station has weather at eighteen minutes into the newscast, sports at twenty-four minutes in, and a newscast that's labeled Action News, Newscenter 4, or Eyewitness News. Maybe that's been the identity of these stations for so long, perhaps twenty years or more, that no one would know them by any other name. As much as WSVN in Miami is held up as a renegade whose tabloid format is spreading, at least they're merciless in cutting stories to just what has to go on the air. The music behind the anchors may be frenetic, the news set's colors may be bold, and the newscasters may be reading at warp speed . . . but if it's winning in the ratings, and can hold the line on truth and fairness, then at least it's trying to break out of the mold.

On the ownership end, I'm glad to see broadcasters and their co-owned newspapers teaming up—WFAA Television with the *Dallas Morning News*, the *Chicago Tribune* and WGN, and the *Tampa Tribune* and WFLA. It's long overdue. Broadcasters and newspaper writers, traditional competitors, are now in the electronic age, and it's time the jealousies and worries about exploitation were put aside. What we need is more common ground where those seventy or seventy-five reporters on a metropolitan daily can provide an up-to-date look for television, including investigative work, and still promote the sale of papers the next morning.

Sometimes I wish I could simply take more time out of the day, wade through perhaps the 40 percent of ad space, and do what we are doing less of each day—read the local newspaper and some national news magazines. Newspapers can give us the depth to many stories, plus that coverage includes everything from real estate to travel destinations, and perhaps most importantly, let us know what kind of job our local government is doing. Newspaper reporting staffs can be larger than those for television simply because of the sheer number of people required to get one TV program on the air is so much greater than what one newspaper reporter with pen in hand can accomplish.

Much has been written about larger and larger broadcasting conglomerates controlling more and more television stations. For radio's part, many markets have ten or twelve stations owned by the same company. I think the bigger worry is for those big conglomerates that don't have broadcasting or cablecasting as their main focus, but control other large businesses. The temptation for them is to look at what the bottom line is, and if they don't happen to be particularly adept at broadcasting, to strip it to the bare bones and finance their other business concerns. That could also lead to their news directors curtailing certain investigative work to protect the other businesses in the corporation.

The fact that a TV station in, say, Greensboro, can look almost identical in its on-air news presentation to a station in San Jose can also defeat the process of stations being in touch with their local communities. That doesn't happen because some news director in Greensboro flies to San Jose and says, "Wow! This place is hot! We need to do more stories on biotech companies and computers!" It happens because a consulting firm finds out what brings in higher ratings in one city, then brings it to another city, no matter what the differences are in the communities.

At KOTV in Tulsa we even did a series on airplane hijackings that was cloned from a series done in Miami. Never mind that there never had been, and probably never would be, an airplane hijacking to Cuba from Tulsa, Oklahoma. Nevertheless, by using our good relationship with the airport manager to ride around on the tarmac, wave at the control tower while shooting some condemning video, we sabotaged his career by pointing out the alleged lack of security. We even put a bunch of engineering tools through the security scanning and metal detector devices, using a tall blonde woman who was interning for us. (She certainly matched the profile of a hijacker.)

Perhaps I remember that series so well because I was the reporter who did the follow-up reports with the irate airport manager. We couldn't even get within one hundred yards of the airport without the threat of being stopped and having our camera dismantled into its smallest components to make sure we took no pictures.

Fortunately, with the passage of time, things changed. Unfortunately for the airport manager, Richard Ballenger, his transfer out of Tulsa was one of the changes. He was a good person, just caught in a TV station's search for ratings.

That search for ratings has always extended to another area where I don't think TV stations should be going: It's the area of demographics. OK, I'm fifty years old, and I realize the ideal demographics for local and national TV advertisers are supposed to be the 18–49 age group, or perhaps even younger, 18–35.

I'm all in favor of targeting people of all ages—young and older, but currently the biggest growth in potential audience is the baby boomer generation. The 35–54 age group will top eighty million by 2001, compared to sixty million for all other demographic groups. By 2011, the oldest members of the baby boomer generation will turn sixty-five, and begin retiring with an average net worth of $222,000. I think it is making the networks, especially CBS, take notice that they can win a ratings sweep (as CBS did in November of 1997) by capturing that 35–54 age segment. So, maybe there is hope for programming for mature audiences, and that's where CNN fits in.

The reality that CNN is wrestling with even today is how do you top yourself when such an event as the Persian Gulf War doesn't come along very often? For the millions of insomniacs we created, and the millions of viewers around the world who bought all those satellite dishes, there was a certain letdown after the Persian Gulf War ended. It was rekindled with the O. J. Simpson Bronco chase, then in August of '97 by Princess Diana's tragic death. Ironically, her death late on a Friday night caught CNN, ABC, NBC, and CBS in a position where it was almost impossible to get videotape of anything other than the crumpled Mercedes for several hours. Paris news crews were off for the weekend, and only small staffs were on duty to start wall-to-wall coverage. At CNN, anchor Linden Soles, whose contract was not renewed by CNN President Rick Kaplan at the end of 1997, provided the calm and conciseness that the story merited. With CNN's correspondent Jim Bitterman interviewing eyewitnesses two hours after the crash, CNN at least had wider coverage of the story than the other networks.

Perhaps one of the most defining moments of the tragedy came with nonstop, emotionally moving video of Princess Diana's funeral. The freelance photographers who had hounded Princess Diana in life had suddenly given way to the mainstream news photographers who gave us the discreet and poignant video of

Elton John's tribute and Diana's brother's speech, while keeping their cameras off her sons, Prince William and Prince Harry during the funeral. Many people are still out there at this moment . . . waiting for the next big drama.

I was asked once in a radio interview what story I thought I had covered the best of the hundreds of stories I had done. I couldn't think of any. In local news at KOTV in Tulsa, I had to come up with something every day or I couldn't justify my presence to the news director. Many times, I took the easy way out. I didn't put in the extra hours that would have made my work excel. I didn't begin each day looking for that interesting angle at a veterans parade or plaque dedication.

When the question is asked, "What story did you cover that you had the most fun doing?" then I have numerous answers. I may not have enlightened the audience, but I tried my hardest to entertain them when given the chance. I roped more goats on TV, rode more circus elephants, and raced more armadillos than you'd care to know about.

I also danced . . . once . . . and believe me, it was unplanned. I was doing a live report one October evening for KOTV's 10:00 P.M. news. I was standing on the stage in front of some three thousand people under a giant tent, enjoying the festivities of Tulsa's Oktoberfest. Many, in fact, had enjoyed the festivity of consuming alcohol probably a little too much, so they were in the mood for a little fun at the drop of the oom-pah-pah bandleader's baton.

Ten o'clock came, the field producer counted me down to the beginning of the live report, and I began to describe the festive atmosphere created, in part, by all that German beer flowing. Then the band began to play.

That was not in my script.

Suddenly a slim young woman, perhaps about twenty-five, with beautiful red hair, appeared in the corner of my eye. I continued talking to the camera. She stepped onto the stage, then in front of me . . . then put her arms to my shoulders . . . and we began dancing!

I was trying to maintain eye contact with the camera in a live report while dancing in circles, hoping that I wouldn't tie myself up in my own microphone cord, or worse, entangle it around my neck.

Fortunately, my dance partner, perhaps in consort with the oom-pah-pah-band, just wanted to have some momentary fun. She vanished from the stage and back into the huge throng just as quickly as she had arrived. I finished my report, then did the only prudent thing.

I grabbed a Lowenbrau and joined the party.

As a postscript, I was sitting a the Full Moon restaurant in Tulsa in 1995, and a vivacious redhead came up to me. She introduced herself as Rita Wood. She admitted she was the one on that stage fourteen years before. We both had a good laugh. The mystery had finally been solved.

I'd like to see more emphasis placed on long-form documentary and investigative programming at CNN. If NBC, with fewer than half the staff members of CNN, can do four entertaining and informative nights of "Dateline NBC," then CNN can do a whole lot more than one hour that vacillates between hard news and outright entertainment ("Impact") on Sunday nights.

Every time I see Bill Kurtis anchoring one of those "Investigative Reports" series on the Arts and Entertainment Network, I think, "Why can't CNN do that?" Now that MSNBC and Fox are gnawing a small, but not insignificant chunk off of CNN's audience, I don't think CNN can afford to simply scrape the surface with three or four-minute summations and call it a day. MSNBC's potential audience is now over forty-two million, and Fox News has an estimated twenty-two million, still well behind the seventy million of CNN and Headline News, but with enough money to force CNN to do better.

The CNN audience averages over forty-seven years of age, and their incomes are above the national average, so it would seem that CNN could produce more high-quality investigative work, or contract it out, and that advertisers would be willing to pay a premium for that kind of programming to air in slow periods such as the weekends and late nights. I think CNN's new chief, Rick

Kaplan, sees that trend, and I predict he's going to develop that kind of programming.

CNN's ratings dipped by one-third over the previous year in the second quarter of 1997, the lowest they'd been since about 1984. By late 1997 and early 1998 the ratings were slowly turning around, thanks to the saber-rattling from Saddam Hussein and the American military buildup in the Persian Gulf. But the drop in ratings always resumes though as soon as the crisis dissipates.

CNN remains a real hit with not only Americans, but the world at large. Yet it had to make a mid-course correction in 1997 in a situation that, had it gone unchecked by the print media, could have put the network in an unfavorable light.

Tom Johnson had okayed CNN anchors and reporters to become movie bit players in a series of 1997 movies, such as *Jurassic Park: The Lost World, Con Air, Face Off,* and *Contact* starring Jody Foster. It was in *Contact* that the line of journalism and movie overkill was clearly crossed. No fewer than eight anchors and reporters, along with CNN talk-show hosts Larry King and Geraldine Ferraro appeared across the wide screen. In one scene a spacecraft blew up behind longtime CNN space analyst John Holliman.

It wasn't really the movie itself that was worrisome, because "Contact" had the high-concept tag that the book's author, Carl Sagan, would have been proud of. My reason for squirming in my theater seat was because I could visualize how the print media reporters might react to CNN clearly going "Hollywood."

They didn't feel too good about it.

From the *Atlanta Journal* to the *San Francisco Chronicle,* CNN's experiment to tap a potentially younger movie-going audience to sample CNN had backfired. Then-CNN President Tom Johnson back-peddled as fast as he could, and I think his damage-control was successful . . . this time. The print media would be alert, though, for any future transgressions.

CNN White House correspondent Wolf Blitzer, who has turned down numerous filmmakers, is among the reporters and anchors such as NBC's Jane Pauley, who have consistently ruled out movies for fear of that credibility issue.

CNN still is unmatched for its integrity and the speed of getting the news out. What is lacking is promoting the true star power of its anchors and reporters. Why are the names of Tom Brokaw, Jane Pauley, and Katie Couric so well-known? Mainly because they are promoted in every way possible. People watch for people they're familiar with. Most people are familiar with certain CNN talent. Larry King is at the top of the list, though his talk show runs the gamut of topics—far beyond news. CNN's Bernie Shaw and Headline News's Lynne Russell are high on the list. Donna Kelly, Leon Harris, and Joie Chen have received a fair amount of promotion, but they could be so much more valuable as household names.

That promotion needs to extend to both CNN-SI (CNN Sports Illustrated, a twenty-four-hour sports stories network, which is simulcast by CNN a total of two and one-half hours a day and provides sports updates twice hourly for Headline News) and CNN-FN (CNN's twenty-four-hour financial network that is simulcast by CNN three hours a day, and provides twice-hourly financial updates for Headline News). And it wouldn't hurt if both operations were jazzed up a bit with better lighting, faster-paced formats, and simply more people to get the job done. ESPN, with its three networks, enjoys a big ratings advantage over CNN-SI, with flashier shows, better remotes, and simply more people to do the job. CNN-FN has run into a similar fate against CNBC, which also does a better job of promoting its people.

One thing that has mystified me about CNN, Headline News, and for that matter local news, is how much promotion goes into weekday anchors versus those on the weekends. Are there no viewers on the weekends? Of course there are, and in fact there are more people watching Headline News Saturday mornings and Sunday nights than almost anytime during the week. People are at home playing with the kids Saturday mornings, and they're home Sunday nights resting up for the work week ahead.

I still believe that CNN and Headline News do the job well when a crisis happens, as exemplified by the huge upward spike in the ratings when you have something on the order of a Persian Gulf War, a Bronco chase, or a verdict in the O. J. Simpson trial, the death of Princess Diana, or a crisis in the White House.

But a crisis doesn't happen every day, or every week.

CNN has fallen from its position as one of the top four cable networks just five years ago (with ESPN, USA, and TBS in that group) to the eleventh highest-rated cable network now. Headline News is nineteenth. And the last year showed the biggest percentage drop so far, from a .7 in 1996 or 450,000 households per quarter hour, to .5 in 1997, or 328,000 households. Headline News saw a similar drop, down to 170,000 households by February of 1998.

Nickelodeon stays at or near the top of the ratings these days, and even Time-Warner's Cartoon Network is ahead of CNN.

There is some bright news: CNN's .5 dwarfs MSNBC's .1, and that's well ahead of the Fox News Network. But it's one-tenth of the rating of ABC, NBC, or CBS, and when you take into consideration that even a .1 change in the ratings is equivalent to about $200 million in ad revenue, it's easy to see why the pressure is on former ABC executive Rick Kaplan, now CNN USA president, to jump-start the ratings.

Kaplan has made a significant start, but he also has to realize that even if he could come away with a $400 million profit in 1998 for CNN and Headline News, he can't expect that to be plowed back in for more equipment, promotion, and big anchor, reporter, and producer salaries. It never has been before, and it is likely that the money will go to support weaker parts of the Time-Warner organization.

Kaplan was given a free hand within the CNN budget to add and subtract people wherever he wanted when he was hired in August of '97. But quickly he set in motion a process that would have huge ramifications, A long-anticipated redo of the CNN newsroom and anchor set, originally priced at three million dollars, soared to over seven million. Within budget-crunching CNN, that expenditure had to be met with cuts somewhere else.

Kaplan also made a move not to renew the contracts of several CNN anchors and reporters: Longtime Detroit and Miami correspondent Robert Vito, former Moscow Bureau Chief Steve Hurst, Atlanta CNN anchors Linden Soles and Kitty Pilgrim, medical correspondent Jeff Levine, New York-based anchor Norma Quarles, "Computer Connection" host and former Tokyo correspondent Brian Nelson, and "Talk Back Live" host Susan Rook. ABC anchor luminaries Judd Rose and Jeff Greenfield were brought in along with a number of new producers, friends of Kaplan during his days at ABC. Willow Bay, the former ABC Sunday Morning anchor, also came over in a rather bizarre scenario. She's the wife of the president of ABC, Bob Iger.

Kaplan is a very hands-on kind of executive, and his style can be abrasive. He was quick to make sure CNN staffers knew that he thought CNN had been outmaneuvered in March of '98 when "60 Minutes" and reporter Ed Bradley had an exclusive interview with Kathleen Willey about her sexual allegations against President Clinton. Kaplan's tirade through the CNN newsroom showed the intensity of the man. That intensity, though, may be his undoing, because it's the antithesis of what Johnson brought to the job, and with employees already wondering whether to stand behind this guy who came over from the competition, Kaplan may never find the welcome mat.

He also has few perks compared to his ABC days. The limos are few and far between. The expansive travel budget he enjoyed at ABC is non-existent at CNN, as are large chunks of money for marketing CNN programming in any other medium.

Numerous head-to-head confrontations between Kaplan and former CNN Executive Vice-President Bob Furnad also seemed to be just over the horizon. When Furnad took over at Headline News in August of '97 from Jack Womack, he immediately broke a cardinal rule—demanding frequent live reports from CNN reporters at the top and bottom of the hour. The reporters balked at spending more time trying to do live reports for not only CNN, but CNN International and now Headline News, making it tough just to go cover the different angles of a story. So Kaplan stepped in and put a stop to 90 percent of it.

But Furnad's aggressiveness may have been more of an attempt to challenge Kaplan's authority rather than just a well-intentioned step to boost Headline News ratings, because the next budget-cutting move was about to hit the Headline News staff right between the eyes in 1998.

The mistakes that had haunted Headline News Executive Vice-President Jon Petrovich in 1996, when 80 of the 260 staffers bailed out rather than put up with massive scheduling and job-description changes, were compounded in May of '98, all in the name of streamlining the operation and saving money. This time the massive cuts fell squarely on the shoulders of Furnad, who had been near the top of the executive hierarchy of CNN since its founding in May of 1980. That was until Kaplan was hired and Furnad was told to go down to Headline News, replace Jack Womack with the newly-formed title of president of Headline News, but keep Womack as his top assistant. Furnad balked at the idea of running a network he considered less than CNN, but played the good soldier rather than face the alternative of a forced retirement.

By the spring of '98, two different consulting teams from outside, both looking at how to cut costs to afford the purchase of the latest digitized AVID equipment to more fully-automate Headline News (and perhaps CNN itself at a later date), recommended massive staff cuts. Furnad early in the year announced that in addition to automating the cameras and eliminating studio camera operators at Headline News, he would also cut out the people who play the tapes (since the AVID AirPlay system computerized the show on servers) and most of the fonters, those people who enter the names and locations for each half-hour's worth of news. That put 20 people out on the street from the 260 Headline News staffers.

Then by late spring the edict came down from Furnad that seventy more people would go by the end of 1998. Interestingly, none of them were from the ever-increasing group of middle management types, many of whom had insulated themselves into areas of "long-range planning" and "evaluating employee performance," if indeed there were to be any employees left to evaluate after the staffing cuts.

Furnad was between a rock and a hard place. He had to go along with the consultants wishes, but he had to know inside that cutting the staff by almost a third could have consequences on the air. Among the seventy who would not be replaced were anchors Lyn Vaughn (who couldn't come to terms on her contract), David Goodnow, and Toria Tolley. Both Vaughn, who did the 11:00 A.M. to 3:00 P.M. EST shift, and Goodnow, who anchored the 11:00 P.M. to 3:00 A.M. EST shift, had been with the network over fourteen years. Toria Tolley, primarily a weekend anchor, had been there for over seven years.

Of the technical and editorial people to be let go, people who had years of experience as copy editors were lost, and just as it happened in 1996, the fear of being fired forced some veterans to look elsewhere instead of waiting around to see who the guillotine would chop next. By mid-1998, it was, as one staffer put it, ". . . like walking into a morgue in that newsroom. If it's not you that's getting cut, it's your buddy."

The master plan revealed by Furnad would, if carried to its conclusion over a period of several months, make Headline News more like the CNN Airport Network, since more than 90 percent of its material is taped, rather than a network of two-thirds live and one-third on tape, which Headline News had been. Instead of fifteen to eighteen stories appearing in the first thirteen-minute segment of each half hour, twenty-five to twenty-eight stories, many of them as short as twenty seconds, with no reporter piece over a minute-twenty, would be recorded by the anchor during the first two hours of an anchor's newly expanded eight-hour shift (previously the shifts were four hours). Then the material would be digitized, loaded into the computer, and the producer-writer teams would try to build a thirteen-minute segment for the top of the hour by adding up all those little pieces. Then, so the theory goes, the little pieces could be shaken up just like a giant jigsaw puzzle, and rearranged for the thirteen-minute segment leading off the bottom of the hour. Much the same format with shorter, headline-only stories, would be used in the feature segments at twenty-four and fifty-four minutes after the hour.

For live, breaking stories (and they can come frequently especially during the daytime hours), overcoming the time constraints of making the live element begin and end in exactly the number of seconds that another two or three stories had previously filled would be a monumental task. The producer had to insert weather reports at eight and thirty-eight minutes past the hour, with no room for the show to bump those times to even nine or thirty-nine minutes past. So the whole idea hinged on worrying more about how much time you had to fit the story in, rather than worrying about the facts or importance of the story itself. Timers on a NASCAR track would have had an easier job.

To add to the frustration of the smaller staff trying to keep up with the assembly-line-type product, the consultants had come up with phrases for the new, younger, and certainly smaller audience of white males aged twenty-four to fifty-three that they were seeking. They called this group the "Time Warriors," who, upon descending into their cubicles wherever they work, could be given the dubious label of "Water-Cooler Smart." How catchy. Perhaps the "Time Warriors" would eventually end up with the same knowledge that the water cooler possessed.

In addition to the attempt to condense details on major stories, as well as the far-from-major stories that would round out the increased story count in those thirteen-minute segments at the top and bottom of the hour, there was also a battle that continued between Furnad and those who wore a few more stripes on their lapels upstairs and in New York.

The largest expenditure from the budget of Headline News in recent years was the outlay for the business news supplied by CNN-FN under Lou Dobbs in New York. Furnad didn't like the idea of having to spend so much on what he felt was not a top quality product, so he told CNN President Tom Johnson he didn't want it anymore. But Dobbs argued that Headline News should be forced to use it, and pay for it. Dobbs won the argument. Furnad cut the segment from three minutes to two as an obvious snub, even though he still pays for it.

With Furnad and Kaplan also on not the best of terms, more salvos are likely to be fired. Early in '98 Kaplan consolidated the tape editing and satellite feeds areas into one centralized point run by CNN staffers. That left Headline News and CNN International, both formerly with their own tape-editing crews in the same building, without the capability of deciding the length or content of the videotape they use on the air. It saves Kaplan money, but for Furnad, who would have had Kaplan's job if the normal hierarchal moves had been followed in '97 at CNN, he can only sit near the water cooler two floors below Kaplan and fume.

5 4 3 2 1

So You Want to Get Ahead in Broadcasting . . .

IF YOU'VE BECOME A JOURNALIST OR ARE THINKING OF becoming one, I congratulate you. I want you to really enjoy the business, and avoid some misconceptions and pitfalls.

First of all, your college degree doesn't have to be in the field of communications or journalism, and I think any degree in languages, sociology, psychology, or history is just as valuable. The key is to get at least a four-year degree in something, then go on for an advanced degree if you have the funds and the even a moderate amount of interest. You'll not only have something that's better than money—because no one can take it away from you—but you'll learn from the people around you in an academic atmosphere. Most importantly to your resume, you'll have that piece of paper that says I did it. I survived it. I just want a little respect.

To be successful and happy in broadcasting as an anchor or reporter, you have to have one quality above all others—you have to like people. There are few skills that demand such intense team-work not only from your coworkers (photographers, editors, assignment editors, producers, directors) to get the news program on the air. There are some tough lessons that you may face: you may get fired for no reason, you may work long hours day after day with your colleagues under deadline pressure, and you may have to survive standing in twenty-degree weather for an hour and a half, waiting for the mayor to come outside his or her toasty little office.

There's also the thing about money and your own personal time. Both will be in short supply in the beginning. If you can accept working for less than $20,000 and find that the Fourth of July, Thanksgiving, and Christmas may not be your days off if they fall on your normal work days, then I think you'll make it.

Local and national TV and radio news can be stressful, but rewarding. I know a lot of on-air personalities who, in a supermarket, run from the very people who watch them, but 99 percent of the time I enjoy being recognized and talking with people.

Radio news also has a lot going for it. I had a whole lot less equipment to drag around in the field, and I generally didn't have to rely on anyone else. I was my own director, editor, reporter, producer, and anchor. I could even wear shorts on the weekends.

The communications industry is full of rapid technological changes that are forcing reporters to know more about both computers and the camera equipment in the field. The starting salary for a TV reporter today is only about $17,000 on average. Then again, there are some monetary goals to aim for. The average salary of a evening or late evening anchor in the top ten markets—that is those cities like Dallas or Atlanta or larger—is $313,000. I thought that would get your attention.

Your dream of becoming a successful journalist shouldn't be shattered by the thought of a low salary right now. The money will come as you gain experience. You will need a basic knowledge of how Spanish and French words are pronounced. More and more, you need to know how to pronounce names like Francois Mitterand, Ernesto Zedillo, and Alija Itzebegovic. If you've got a problem with names, the audience won't believe you, because they've heard those names pronounced correctly by the many media organizations out there.

Stay informed on current events. History courses can also be valuable, no matter whether it's ancient Egyptian history or World

War II history. Look toward the future too, and stay computer literate.

If you're living in your hometown and loving it—as I did in Tulsa, Oklahoma—and you don't want to move, think it over. Tulsa, to cite one example, is a wonderful city with very caring people who won't ever forget you. That's a huge plus. Chances are, though, that a move out of your current job will eventually be forced on you. That is, you can easily be taken for granted and remain underpaid, or a new news director can come in and clean house. If you're feeling underutilized right now in your current position, and you've tried unsuccessfully to move up within the station, chances are it won't get better, it will get worse.

Being an anchor or reporter may not be your style. Producers, assignment editors, camera operators, and computer-savvy types are in many cases in higher demand in the broadcasting world simply because of the huge numbers of on-air people out there. At CNN, one fast-growing area is CNN Interactive, where everything from live shows to "Larry King Live" to "Burden of Proof" are being put on the web. In fact, CNN Interactive programmers, who enter the video and text on CNN's four websites, are in such demand from other companies that CNN has trouble keeping them.

I know some of you would probably like to report or anchor for CNN some day. Here's how: *Pay your dues.* Get a job as a reporter for a local station, then start moving up the ladder to a better position there, or another larger local station. If you still have that drive to be at CNN in about three or four years, use an agent or your own persistence to get to know the people at the top of CNN and Headline News. Right now that's Rick Kaplan at CNN, and Bob Furnad at Headline News, both in Atlanta. CNN Human Resources screens applicants for all kinds of jobs, and if Kaplan and Furnad can't see you, ask them to at least look at your tape or suggest that their assistants do it. Sounds too simple, doesn't it? Well, sometimes the simple way is the best way.

Ninety-five percent of the anchors and reporters at both CNN and Headline News are not people who started in the mailroom, or the assignment desk, or as executive producers, and worked their way up within Turner Broadcasting. CNN and Headline News are structured so that anchors are on one side of the equation, and everybody else is on the other—*and the two shall almost never meet.* It would be nice if that weren't so, but anchors are generally expected to read what's on the teleprompter, ad lib in crisis situations, then go home.

It could be a whole lot worse, since at Headline News you anchor four hours on a single shift, then you get in your car and drive home. I liked that part, but I'll admit that one reason I enjoyed local television was the chance to cover a major breaking story.

If you decide you want a higher-paying, higher-profile job in San Diego, Boston, or New York, then get moving. I'd recommend looking around for an agent who truly believes in you, has connections, and also has a good track record for honesty. Also, try to get a list of at least some of the agent's clients, then look at the list closely, because you want someone who isn't overloaded with people in your particular area of expertise. A good agent can be invaluable if they stay in contact with news directors and general managers around the country, keep hunting for the kind of job *you* want, and keep you informed frequently about where your tapes are being sent. As you go higher up the ladder and get more perks or extra goodies in your contract, an agent can even act as a buffer between you and management on sensitive issues.

Remember that agents have their own priorities. I flew in to see an agent in Chicago one day, and discovered that despite my prior arrangements with him, he only had fifteen minutes before his tee time on a local golf course. So I sat there and watched him work on the phone. He had two phones going, one by each ear. On one line he had an executive in San Diego who wanted one of his clients for their 11:00 P.M. news, but the agent wanted that person to accept a job in Dallas, and had another guy in mind for the San Diego job. Neither of the clients probably ever knew what was being said behind the scenes. I didn't sign with him.

Put your tapes in the hands of several prospective agents, then go see them in person just like you would a news director. The money you spend traveling to talk to agents is invaluable, because you'll probably come away liking the agent more, or wondering why you ever went to see them in the first place. Some agents are great at the bargaining table, justifying their 10 percent cut of your salary and much more. Other agents, an even rarer breed, will hunt and hunt to find the kind of job that fits your skills with a station's needs. A few agents give the good ones a bad name. They'll fool you into thinking they're looking day and night, and that if you sign a three-year agreement to have them as your exclusive agent, they'll deliver Los Angeles or New York for you. Then, once they've got you on the dotted line, they can concentrate on their more high-priced talent that will bring them bigger fees, and you'll get a job only if it falls in their lap.

I've had contracts with two agents in my career. The first one, Sherlee Barish, wanted to move me around the country so I could get a track record of bringing up the ratings in places like Altoona, Pennsylvania, and Florence, South Carolina. I just didn't have the overwhelming desire to work in either place at the time, so I eventually left her. The second agent, Conrad Shadlen, was well worth the 10 percent I paid him each year of my original three-year agreement with Headline News. I got a so-called boiler-plate agreement that looked the same for just about everyone else who anchored there at the time, but at least it got me on the staff.

If you're ready to look for a job, and you don't have an agent, or don't want to depend solely on the one you've got, develop a relationship over the phone with news directors or their assistants. Find out more about the city and the stations that you're going to look at. What's the latest debate in the city council or school board? Who are the movers and shakers in that community? It gives you, first of all, a chance to have something to talk to that news director about that will show them you do your homework.

Secondly, you want to know how well that station may pay, who owns it, and if they're a solid owner. Has it been a leader in news for many years? Is there a lot of turnover among personnel?

I dropped in on a friend of mine who was reporting at KDFW, then the CBS affiliate in Dallas in the mid-80s. I wasn't even looking for a job. I was just visiting my friend in the newsroom. In the hour and a half that I sat there, one female reporter and the news director had a huge verbal blowup behind the picture window of the news director's office, and two employees who didn't even know me came up and told me that I shouldn't ever even think of working there. Scratch that one off the potential list.

The wide range of stories you've written as a producer or your series of reports on about corruption at city hall won't get you very far if you just send out your tapes helter-skelter. Read the trade publications like *Electronic Media* for jobs. Get on the Internet at www.tvspy.com to access Don Fitzpatrick Associates' "Shoptalk" daily news update on the broadcast and cable industry, which is based in San Francisco and published daily. Don is the guy that many stations call when they want a tape of perhaps fifty people to look at and potentially hire, and you can correspond with his "Shoptalk" daily through various on-line services. He also has an excellent booklet with names, addresses, and facts about various agents.

Firms like Audience Research and Development in Dallas, Frank Magid in Marion, Iowa, and Broadcast Image Consultants in San Antonio have a clientele of probably over 350 TV stations between the three of them. Send them your tape. It doesn't cost anything to be placed in their files, and they'll probably know about job openings at stations days, if not weeks, before you will.

It may seem obvious, but if you don't have an answering machine, get one. Many news directors may call only once if that phone just keeps on ringing. If they do get an outgoing message, my guess (after talking to about 150 news directors over the years) is that the stresses of the job can frequently limit their sense of humor. They don't want to hear any long, obnoxious tones, or your attempt to imitate Clint Eastwood.

A fax machine, E-mail, and a website can also be valuable. I have them, and I wouldn't want to be without any of them for the speed of communication with all the people who you just can't get over the phone. As more and more computers become capable of downloading audio and video in shorter and shorter periods of time, news directors will be more impressed with the applicant whose bio and tape can be downloaded in about the time it takes the news director to open the applicant's resume packet.

When you find out a station has an opening, you want your resume and tape to already be finished and ready for mailing, or better yet, taken personally to that news director. Let me give a little hint on what *not* to put on your resume page (I stress *page* here). I don't recommend a second page, since it can get lost.

Don't give a temporary address and a permanent address. News directors don't have time to decide which one is the real one.

Do include three or four references on your resume, and by all means let them know they may be called.

Don't lie. Honesty impresses news directors. If something didn't work out with you and a previous employer, you're in the majority, so admit it. Probably 60 percent of the people in broadcasting get fired or trimmed due to downsizing at one time or another.

Don't send an eight-by-ten glossy. Force the news director to look at your tape, not your picture. Besides, if they don't like your glossy photo, they may draw devil's ears and goatees on it and pin it to the bulletin board.

Don't use the current station's letterhead for your cover letter. You'll look like you're trying to find a new job on your current employer's time.

Don't send out a letter to a news director without being sure you have the correct spelling and full title of that person. I've even forgotten to date my letters at the top, then had the news director point out that the letter came to his or her office undated.

Finally, even if you don't have the remotest interest in working for a station after you've interviewed with them, do me one favor. Sit down and write them a thank you letter, and put it in the mailbox the first thing the next morning. News directors, as well as anchors like me who take the time to respond to inquiries, remember that sort of thing.

A word now on reporter audition tapes. There's nothing wrong with an anchor or reporter stand-up montage at the beginning of the tape. A combination of five categories—a stand-up from a serious piece, a humorous piece, a series segment, a set piece, and a *live* shot can get that news director's attention. Just don't let the whole montage drift beyond a minute and fifteen seconds. Variety and brevity are the keys.

If you're auditioning for an anchor slot, put a couple of edited-down casts back-to-back, concentrating on including chitchat between you and your co-anchor, weathercaster, or sportscaster. These two portions of an edited cast should run no more than ten minutes, followed by any *live* or reporting pieces, not to exceed six minutes. Put your work on VHS, beta, and three-quarter inch tapes, then find out each news director's preference for a tape format before you send the tape. I'm still awaiting that day, hopefully soon, when all reporters looking for work will have web sites, and downloading from the news director's office will simplify the procedure greatly.

By the way, for sportscasters, the interaction with other members of the anchor team is a must on the tape. Do some hard news. Giving scores is not really brain surgery, so if you've got a story that involves taking a stand on something, or explaining what's wrong with a sports program in your community, you've got the perfect entree to the news director's pulse.

In weathercasting, put a tape together with a weathercast from a severe weather day and one from a cheery weather day. If you've done anything even close to environmental reporting, include it on the tape. Don't forget to put the tosses between yourself and the news anchors on the tape too.

I've been where you are right now. I've had news directors send me rejection letters with the admonition not to send any more. Worse, I've had them ask me if I've considered another career.

I've had news directors send me other people's tapes in the mail. Reporters and anchors have called me to say they've gotten some of mine. Over the years, I sent out over three hundred tapes, and one reason they got mixed up was generally because I failed to put my name, address, and phone number not only on the tape, but on the side and front of the tape box. I also found that as the years went on, fewer tapes were returned to me. News directors were simply too overloaded with everyday work to return them all. So don't take that little slight as any kind of rejection.

One great development over the past two years has been the huge growth in web sites on the Internet by not only consulting firms like Audience Research and Development in Dallas, but by agents and individuals alike. It means that all those tapes being mailed from job seekers to consultants, and from consultants to their station clients, will become a thing of the past over the next five years. Right now consulting firms still don't have the space and time to digitize every one of thousands of audition tapes into streaming video, but rapid technological changes will allow that in the coming years.

The Napoli Management Group early in 1998 became the first on-air talent representation firm to feature videos of clients' work on the Internet. The firm's president, Mendes Napoli, has within his organization, over two hundred clients. It makes it easy for news directors and general managers to access a web site, in this case www.tvtalent.com and access not only a video clip of the anchor or reporter's current work, but still pictures and resumes as well. As newcasters become computerized, and reports and voice-overs are played from a disc or hard drive, then recorded in their final live on-air version as well, you'll be able to edit and send your audition material from your computer to the website of the agent or consultant, with no audition tape involved.

Things can and do go wrong when you are out there trying to find a job, so maybe the following story will keep things in perspective. I had a job right in the palm of my hand in 1980, and I let it slip through my fingers in an inexcusable way.

I had been talking to a Las Vegas television station's news director about a main anchor slot that was soon going to open up. The news director was all pumped up about hiring me, and the money was good. He said he would have to get one final okay from the general manager before making a final decision, but he pointed out that the current anchor didn't know he was about to be fired.

So I called a good friend of mine, Watson Jelks, a disc jockey at a radio station in Las Vegas who I'd worked with on the morning shift at KRMG in Tulsa. Watson was on the air the morning I called, and happy to hear from me. I told him of the possibility that I might be taking a job out there, and gave him details about the station itself. I even asked him if he'd heard anything bad or good about the station. He said he hadn't.

Then he broke away for a moment to do an announcement on the air, and put me on hold. When he came back about a minute later we finished our conversation with the thought that we'd have to get together when this deal was signed and I moved out there.

The Las Vegas news director was supposed to call within a week, but he didn't. After ten days I called him, and what I heard on the phone that day you wouldn't expect from a group of sailors.

The news director was livid. He was cussing up a storm.

Apparently my good friend Watson, in his haste to welcome his little buddy from Tulsa, had gone on the air while I was on the phone and told the entire Las Vegas metropolitan area that this TV station had hired me, and if he had anything to do with it, there would be a parade for me right down the center of town.

While I had been on hold with Watson, I wasn't hearing any of this rah-rah speech that was actually my funeral dirge.

But that's not all. Not only had the news director barely missed a telephone pole with his car while listening to Watson unknowingly sabotage an entire news operation, the main anchor he was about to fire was listening as well. His car took a header off an embankment, ending up in a ditch. Fortunately, he survived, at least physically. The shock at the news, though, had to be traumatic.

And surprise, surprise. I wasn't going to be hired. Perhaps I might get shot though, if I ever crossed the city limits of Las Vegas.

So that's my lesson that perhaps you can benefit from. If it's a sensitive matter, keep it completely quiet . . . and definitely away from disc jockeys who are on the air.

Now, back to the matter of audition tapes. If humanly possible (and I realize many times it can't be done), take your audition tape personally to the news director's office if you can drive or fly there. Believe me, I know it's costly, but sending them out helter-skelter is almost a guarantee that they will be placed like a small flat stone in what looks like a very tall Leaning Tower of Pisa in a corner of the news director's office, and the clean-up crew won't even be able to reach the top of the stack to dust your little tape.

Trust your own instincts when it comes to agents. If your agent wants you locked into a contract with him or her for three years, and you don't like the way that feels, work out a compromise. These things aren't written in stone. The same thing applies when you or your agent negotiates with a station. Have some options in your mind. Maybe you'll take less money if you can get a shorter contract. Maybe the only market you'd consider, after moving to Memphis, would be a top twenty, or one of the twenty largest metropolitan areas or markets in America. You might work on getting an out, to let you get *out* of the contract with thirty days notice for a job offer in a top twenty market.

You may be surprised what can be put into a contract that makes both sides happy. Just don't take verbal promises. Problems have occurred during my career when a general manager went back on his word, and who's to say the news director who makes that promise that you'll be promoted in six months will be employed there when the time comes.

Get it in writing. In 1979, I signed a five-year agreement with KOTV in Tulsa. It had minuscule pay raises built in. Two years later, only by going to the mat with the threat of resignation did I get a three-year deal with some reasonable raises built in. Obviously, don't threaten to leave unless you either really want to leave, or you just can't tolerate being underpaid and undervalued.

I actually enjoyed being flown around the country to audition for TV reporter and anchor jobs. I was in Greensboro, Scranton, Tucson, Greenville, Jacksonville, Los Angeles, Cincinnati, and Houston on job auditions. Even if I didn't get a job offer, it gave me a little more confidence for the next time I went to audition.

My first chance to make an upward move was in 1977 to KTRK television, the ABC affiliate in Houston. I had been at KOTV in Tulsa for only a year, and went to Houston for an interview. Here I was on what seemed like a blind date, because in auditioning, you never know what awaits you. In this case, the news director sized me up in half-an-hour, and sent me to lunch on my own at the four-stool company snack shop. Sitting by me on the second stool from the left was a twenty-five-year engineering department veteran of the station. We discussed the intriguing and exciting aspects of low-light level characteristics of Ikegami cameras.

Then we ate our hot dogs.

I spent the next two hours until my plane flight took off, wandering through the newsroom like a plague, inflicting myself on any poor soul who had a deadline to meet. Finally, the news director emerged from his office, shook my hand, pointed to the front door and the waiting cab, and mumbled something about "good luck with your career."

I was not impressed. Obviously, neither was he. Just like a *bad* blind date.

A year later, I arrived for an audition in Scranton, Pennsylvania, at the Wilkes-Barre airport. Apparently, the brass band to announce my arrival was taking the day off. A lone ticketing agent, feet propped up on the counter, was asleep. I noticed him only because he was snoring softly. Evidently business was a little slow.

My ride to the TV station was equally uneventful. Lots of old gray and brown buildings. Through the fog, I saw the station. It had these huge spires on top and looked kind of like a church. I was led into the basement of a girls preparatory school. I entered the subterranean world, almost expecting to see the Phantom of the Opera. Bare light bulbs hung from the high ceilings—a perfect setting for an Edgar Allen Poe story.

I entered the anchor studio. It looked the size of two phone booths . . . maybe. The weather map was roughly the size of a single page of the *Rand McNally Road Atlas*. No use asking for the camera and prompter to be moved closer. There was one setting . . . close. The dimensions of the anchor desk resembled a small card table.

Then the *coup de grace*. The attractive co-anchor, in her mid-twenties, turned to me during a break in the audition and asked, "What do you think of this place? You know, I had an offer to anchor weekends in Houston about a month ago. But when I asked my news director what I should do, he said to stay here. He thinks I need another couple of years of seasoning. What do you think?"

The thought hung in the musty air of that basement.

I stared back, trying to appear like I was waiting for the rest of the thought. What could I tell her? The truth? The truth would be to get moving, and don't stop at the airport because it may take too long to wake up the ticket agent!

I kept my mouth shut, and I probably did the right thing for once.

I was eventually offered twice the money I was making in Tulsa to come to Scranton. It taught me a lesson not to assume that market size has everything to do with pay scales. Maybe my female co-anchor in the audition was already making some great money, and spending it enjoying the skiing in the Poconos. I didn't take the job by the way.

Of all the places I went to audition, the biggest was KTTV, an independent station then owned by Metromedia Broadcasting in Los Angeles. I arrived at LAX, and was immediately whisked away to the Los Angeles Sports Arena to do my own version of a stand-up that the station's reporter had just finished. Suddenly, the KTTV reporter was called back to the station, and I was told to accompany the photographer to Terminal Island, where a U.S.

Coast Guard ship was about to dock with a huge marijuana cache, seized just off the coast.

I did an interview with a Coast Guard lieutenant, did a stand-up, got plenty of shots of the ship and the marijuana, and headed back for Hollywood. Then it occurred to me—I was doing the lead story for that night's newscast!

Never mind that I was under contract in Tulsa. Never mind that I came to Los Angeles simply to audition. The lead story for the 10:00 P.M. news was also going to be my audition tape!

That night the report aired, and the next morning the news director was effusive in his praise. He'd hire me, if I could get out of my contract in Tulsa.

"Would KTTV put it in writing?" I asked.

No, they would not. Of course not. They didn't want to be accused of tampering with a contract employee.

So it was like a catch-22, and I had put myself in the position of being fired if anyone among the several hundred thousand viewers had called my boss in Tulsa. I should have demanded a top-twenty out in my KOTV contract, to allow me to move to a much bigger market. It was no one's fault but my own. I did get such an out in my contract a year later.

It reminded me of another mistake I almost made back in 1969. I tell this story here in hopes that you will know that it can happen to you.

When I got the job offer at CKLW in Detroit in 1969, I couldn't wait to hit the road in my 1962 Mercury Comet and put that little station with that two-and-a-quarter-an-hour wage in my rear view mirror. I was going to give KAKC one week's notice and blow that pop stand.

Fortunately, Jim Peters, a wise disc jockey who had been a newsman himself, advised me to be polite, give *two* weeks notice, and keep any stupid remarks about management to myself.

I followed his advice, thankfully.

Two years later I was calling KAKC, asking to come back home, and they were kind enough to take me back, even with the understanding that I'd move again if I found a better wage.

Now for one final thought. If you are fortunate enough to get the kind of job offer that moves you up the ladder in this broadcasting business, and you can take it without throwing your family or your pocketbook into chaos, follow what your heart really desires. You may want to think about Billy Joel's song, "My Life." Many people in this world are hamstrung because they're constantly being told not to step out of line, to play it safe, to stay right where they are, and not to go ahead with their own life. The majority of young people coming into this broadcast journalism business can't afford to stay in the same position or the same town forever, or they risk sliding backward, stifling their growth, and perhaps being replaced by someone who will work for less. Many times they get in a rut and accept it for so long, they don't even know they're in it.

I acted on my chance to expand my horizons, and with a minimum of talent, and a maximum of perseverance, I've done okay. You can do even better.

CHAPTER NINETEEN

The Secret to Your Success

I SOMETIMES WONDER IF I'M ANY GOOD AT GIVING advice or motivation. I know a certain amount about cancer. And, I'm outspoken in advising people on career moves. But what I wanted to include are a few excerpts from a speech I gave to an Alberquerque, New Mexico, group, "People Living through Cancer" in February 1998. It was one of those pieces of writing that's supposed to flow smoothly, and perhaps be heard rather than read. But I still strongly believe in what I told the audience:

> What are the so-called secrets to being successful with both your personal and professional life? For one thing, it's knowing what you want out of life, changing your goals as you change your own needs and desires, and a lot of understanding. This applies to all of us, no matter what our age.
>
> It's a matter of accepting that you will have ups and downs that you sometimes have no control over, and that some people will help you, while others will fail you. To stay with a positive frame of mind no matter what hits you between the eyes is the key. Adversity either makes us bitter and weaker, or challenged and stronger. If all we do is go around blaming our childhood, our

parents, or that unlucky break in the junior year of college, misery will follow us like a junkyard dog, always nipping at our heels.

You are a unique individual. Your life experiences make you one-of-a-kind. There are probably some wonderful hidden qualities inside you, that if you let them come out, will make you feel every day that you're an important part of this world.

There's a line from an old Beatles' song that never is far from my mind. It says "The love you take is equal to the love you make." It's true. People will respond to the way you care about them. How many people do you run into who want to tell you all their problems, and then ask some meaningful, sincere questions about your life? Maybe not as many as you'd like. We get wrapped up in trying to look only at how crazy our own lives have become, usually dwelling on the negative, and never sincerely inquire of others how their lives are going.

Many times the only response we make to someone's long litany about how their problems are almost insurmountable is to change the subject. Again, I think of "the love you take is equal to the love you make." Why not just listen when a person airs their problems? No rebuttal, just listen.

What you may not hear is the "love you make" (by listening silently), translates to "the love you take," because that person who spilled his or her guts to you will be thinking, "You know, that person is really caring. They took the time to listen and weren't judgmental. I want to get to know them better." Yet all you did was listen. It's the beginning of the love that is in almost every heart—the "giving" if you will—starting to flow back to you.

I then continued to talk to the audience about cancer survivors, people in cancer treatment, their families and care-givers, about Oklahoma humorist and just an incredibly knowledgable guy, Will Rogers. He was born about forty miles east of Tulsa in Indian territory at Ologah, Oklahoma. Over the years, I have heard his son refer many times to Will's famous comment that "he never met a man he didn't like."

How could anyone *never* meet a man he didn't like? It could be a matter of attitude. I have interviewed all forms of human life, from convicted murderers, to overpaid entertainers, to politicians caught with their pants down, literally. Very few ever gave me the impression that if I pushed the right buttons and got a dialogue going, that a real human being with real feelings wasn't in there somewhere. It might take a lot of time—perhaps more than I wanted to spend—but likable qualities were there if I had the patience to listen for them.

All too often in this world we give up on people because the person we see on first impression is under pressure, has problems at home, has built up a wall against society, and may have financial and health problems we can hardly fathom. I look at that person as a challenge.

We've all heard the expression of the glass being half-full to some people and half-empty to others. In the restaurant of life, I look at the half-empty glass that the other person has, then pretend I'm pouring my half-full glass in theirs, in the form of positive thoughts, and then take a look at what we've got. They'll invariably be unable to look at the glass the same way again.

I can't truly remember with any feeling of anger the *negative* things that have happened to me in my life. It's not that my memory is failing me. It's just that the good in being alive every day makes everything else seem insignificant in comparison.

I remember 1985 distinctly—the testicular cancer, the three operations, the three sessions of chemotherapy—but I honestly would have to be hooked up to a heart monitor to tell if my pulse

Mom with me at my fiftieth birthday party in Tulsa, May 1997.

quickens whenever that bump in the road of my life is brought up in conversation. I'm simply too busy thinking about what I'm going to do today . . . and then tomorrow . . . and then next year.

I then paused to tell the group about all the fun times I had growing up and going to Edison High School in Tulsa, and going on that first date in my parent's Ford Fairlane 500.

We've all got at least some happy memories. I firmly believe that each of us is a unique human being, even though in today's society we're inundated with pressures to conform. If I were content to follow along blindly behind all the people who never make waves, never take a chance, never take a step out of synch with the others, then I wouldn't be me.

If you're sitting there, saying you'd like to change your life, but the timing is just not right, I've got this late-breaking bulletin for you: Take a chance. Whatever happens, embrace a positive meaning from it, knowing it has helped mold you into a new and improved version of *who you really want to be.*

The time may never be perfectly right, but the clock is ticking on your time on this earth. We dream of doing things like vacations, getting more education, or perhaps raising a family, but we finally run out of time for doing all those things.

Are you thinking of going out and getting a better job? Are you thinking of traveling somewhere that you've always wanted to go? As I have found out, the only risks that you'll ever regret are the ones you didn't take.

I took a risk in deciding to pack my bags in 1985 and go to CNN. I left my friends, my mother, and my local TV audience to take a chance in Atlanta. But I seldom felt alone. I toured six hundred groups of people through the CNN facilities. I have made over fifty flights back to Tulsa to see everyone back there. It was the best of both worlds, and just as it happened in Tulsa when I left KOTV, another door opened as the other closed at Headline News. It was time to get my eggs out of one basket and scatter them among many baskets.

That's a little of my philosophy. Now, I want to just say "thank you" for joining me in this journey down the winding path of broadcasting. Here I am, looking back from afar at my career. My two cats, Blackster and Grey Cakes, are pretty good at standing on the keyboard of this computer and trying to help me with word processing. They're also wonderful company.

Some nights I lie awake, just as I did when I was a youngster, listening to the owls talking to each other. Some days I take about an hour out and go down and feed the ducks, geese, and swans on the seventeen-acre lake that borders my property.

The two full-grown swans generally spot me heading to the lake about twenty yards before I get to the water's edge. If I'm not putting cracked corn in their feed dish on the dock by the time they mentally count to three, they're determined to find out what my problem is.

It's likely that you and I have spent a lot of time together over the years. I shared with you the latest on the Space Shuttle Challenger explosion, the fall of the Berlin Wall, the rescue of Baby Jessica, and much more.

I hope we get to meet again. Until then, I wish you all life's best.